IMAGES OF WAR

Hitler's Defeat on the Eastern Front 1943-1945

Rare Photographs from Wartime Archives

Ian Baxter

Pen & Sword
MILITARY

First published in Great Britain in 2009 by
PEN & SWORD MILITARY
An imprint of
Pen & Sword Books Ltd
47 Church Street
Barnsley
South Yorkshire
S70 2AS

ISBN 978 1 84415 977 2

A CIP catalogue record for this book is
available from the British Library

Typeset by Phoenix Typesetting, Auldgirth, Dumfriesshire
Printed and bound in Great Britain by CPI UK

Pen & Sword Books Ltd incorporates the Imprints of
Pen & Sword Aviation, Pen & Sword Family History, Pen & Sword Maritime,
Pen & Sword Military, Wharncliffe Local History, Pen & Sword Select,
Pen & Sword Military Classics, Leo Cooper, Remember When, Seaforth Publishing
and Frontline Publishing

For a complete list of Pen & Sword titles please contact
PEN & SWORD BOOKS LIMITED
47 Church Street, Barnsley, South Yorkshire, S70 2AS, England
E-mail: enquiries@pen-and-sword.co.uk
Website: www.pen-and-sword.co.uk

Contents

Introduction 4

Photographic Acknowledgements 5

The Author 6

Chapter One
Kursk 7

Chapter Two
Fighting Withdrawal 38

Chapter Three
Winter Warfare 67

Chapter Four
Bagration and Aftermath 96

Chapter Five
Last Battles 105

Appendices 139

Appendix One
Waffen-SS Weapons and Equipment 141

Appendix Two
Infantry Division 1944 145
  The Panzergrenadier Division 1944 145
  Panzer/Panzergrenadier Brigade July 1944 146
  Wehrmacht Division HQ 147

Appendix Three
Combat Uniforms of the Waffen-SS 1943–1945 148

Appendix Four
Combat Uniforms of the Wehrmacht 1943–1945 152
  Ranks 157

Introduction

Hitler's defeat on the Eastern Front is a unique insight into the last two years of the Wehrmacht and Waffen-SS at war. It describes how Hitler's once vaunted force played a decisive role in trying to stem the might of the Russian Army following its defeat at Kursk in the summer of 1943. Drawing on some 250 rare and previously unpublished photographs accompanied by in-depth captions and accompanying text, the book describes how the Wehrmacht and Waffen-SS franticly fought a desperate battle in the face of over-whelming enemy firepower. Despite the adverse situation in which the German Army was placed, soldiers continued to fight to the death in a bitter and frantic struggle to prevent the Red Army from reaching the frontiers of the Reich. Deluged by an armada of tanks, mass infantry assaults, and the constant hammer blows of Russian artillery the German Army along with its fanatic SS counterparts fought a series of vicious battles through the Baltic States, Byelorussia, and then built up new defences along the Vistula in Poland. But as the final months of the war were played out on the Eastern Front, the German Army, with diminishing resources, withdrew across a scarred and devastated Reich to frantically fight out the last battles around the devastated capital of Berlin.

Photographic Acknowledgements

It is with the greatest pleasure that I use this opportunity on concluding this book to thank those who helped make this volume possible. My expression of gratitude first goes to my photographic collector Michael Cremin. He has been an unfailing source; supplying me with a number of photographs that were obtained from numerous private sources.

In Poland I am also extremely grateful to Marcin Kaludow, my Polish photographic specialist, who supplied me with a variety of photographs that he sought from private photographic collections in Poland.

Finally, I wish to display my kindness and appreciation to my American photographic collector, Richard White, who supplied me with a number of rare unpublished photographs.

The Author

Ian Baxter is a military historian who specialises in German twentieth century military history. He has written more than twenty books including *'Wolf' Hitler's Wartime Headquarters, Poland – The Eighteen Day Victory March, Panzers In North Africa, The Ardennes Offensive, The Western Campaign, The 12th SS Panzer-Division Hitlerjugend, The Waffen-SS on the Western Front, The Waffen-SS on the Eastern Front, The Red Army At Stalingrad, Elite German Forces of World War II, Armoured Warfare, German Tanks of War, Blitzkrieg, Panzer-Divisions At War, Hitler's Panzers, German Armoured Vehicles of World War Two, Last Two Years of the Waffen-SS At War, German Soldier Uniforms and Insignia, German Guns of the Third Reich, Defeat to Retreat: The Last Years of the German Army At War 1943–1945, Biography of Rudolf Hoss, Operation Bagration – the destruction of Army Group Centre*, and most recently *The Afrika-Korps*. He has written over one hundred journals including *' Last days of Hitler, Wolf's Lair, Story of the V1 and V2 Rocket Programme, Secret Aircraft of World War Two, Rommel At Tobruk, Hitler's War With His Generals, Secret British Plans To Assassinate Hitler, SS At Arnhem, Hitlerjugend, Battle Of Caen 1944, Gebirgsjäger At War, Panzer Crews, Hitlerjugend Guerrillas, Last Battles in the East, Battle of Berlin,* and many more. He has also reviewed numerous military studies for publication and supplied thousands of photographs and important documents to various publishers and film Production Companyies worldwide.

Chapter One

Kursk

On 5 July 1943, both the *Wehrmacht* and their *Waffen-SS* counterparts stood poised ready to go into action, the pre-dawn light was shattered by a massive German bombardment. The artillery barrage was so intense that in no less than one hour German gunners had hurled more shells than they had used in both Poland and the Western campaigns put together. Despite this violent bombardment, Soviet artillery responded with equal ferocity that soon confirmed what all Germans feared: the attack was not a surprise. All over the front, Soviet artillery crews fired at known German artillery positions that caught the German gunners in the open.

Within hours of the artillery bombardment, three *Waffen-SS* divisions were engaged in the opening stages of the greatest armoured clash in history. The task of the *SS.Panzer-Korps* was to advance via Beresov and Sadeynoye, and breaking through the first defensive belt. Between Lutchki and Jakovlevo was the second line of Russian defensive positions, and when these were destroyed the advance would follow in a general northeastern direction. For this operation the *167.Infanterie*-Division would form part of the *SS Korps* and would guard the left flank.

The 'Leibstandarte's' first attack went well, and their armour soon encircled enemy units that were destroyed with supporting grenadiers. The 9.*Kompanie* of the 'Leibstandarte's' 2.*SS.Panzergrenadier*-Regiment captured two hills west of Byelgorod and took five fortified positions with explosive charges. The soldiers of the 'Totenkopf' division too wasted no time and smashed onto a series of strong Soviet defence lines. At the same time the 'Das Reich' division made considerable progress, and infiltrated enemy lines in front of them.

By evening of the first day of the attack 'Totenkopf', with its new Tiger tanks leading the advance had reached the second Russian defensive belt and managed to capture the village of Yakhontovo and taken an important command post of the Soviet 69th Army. Both the 'Leibstandarte' and 'Das Reich' had done equally as well. With their Tigers and Panzer.IV's they had penetrated some 13 miles into the Russian defences.

By 7 July, the advance of the *Wehrmacht* and *Waffen-SS* seemed more promising

Two photographs showing a halftrack Sd.Kfz.251 carrying Waffen-SS troops to the front during the opening stages of the Kursk offensive, 'Operation Citadel' in early July 1943. In front of the Soviet defensive fortress at Kursk stood the cream of all the German combat formations.

than ever. German forces had managed to smash its way through more than 30 miles of Russian line, whilst in some areas they were equally successful despite enduring bitter fighting. German battle reports confirmed that given the amount of Soviet prisoners taken and the damage inflicted on their lines, it appeared that the Germans were poised on the edge of victory. However, they had not even yet encountered the main enemy positions. The fact that they had advanced at such speed had enabled the Russians to take full advantage of attacking the German flanks.

The initial phase of the Soviet defensive action at Kursk was often crude, messy and costly, but in a tactical and operational sense it achieved its objectives. During the days that followed the Red Army, despite continuing to incur huge losses in both men and weaponry, deprived the Germans of even tactical superiority. Against the *Wehrmacht* and *Waffen-SS* they constantly strengthened their defences through reinforcement, skilfully deploying mobile armour and anti-tank reserves to compensate for the high losses. Within days the Russians had managed to ground down many of the *Wehrmacht* units, including those in the *SS.Panzer-Korps*, and threw its offensive timetable completely off schedule. It was here on the blood-soaked plains at Kursk that for the first time in the war the Red Army had

Waffen-SS machine-gun squad in a trench during 'Citadel'. These troops belong to the II.SS Panzer-Korps which comprised of three premier Waffen-SS divisions, I.SS.Leibstandarte Adolf Hitler Division, the 2.SS Das Reich Division and the 3.SS Totenkopf Division.

Waffen-SS MG 42 machine gunners in a Russian farmstead during the battle at Kursk. At their starting positions, the three SS divisions covered a sector that was 12-miles wide. The Totenkopf occupied the left flank of the advance, the Leibstandarte was in the centre and Das Reich held the right.

savagely contested every foot of ground and was finally on an equal footing. Through sheer weight of Soviet strength and stubborn combat along an ever-extending front, the German mobile units were finally being forced to a standstill.

On 9 July, the *SS.Panzer-Korps* renewed their offensive against very strong enemy forces. In the vicious battle that ensued, the *SS* received a series of sustained attacks, but fanatically held their ground. Although they were in danger of being cut-off and encircled, they received orders to push forward and attack Soviet troops northeast of Beregovoy. During the advance, '*Das Reich*' guarded the eastern flank of '*Totenkopf*' and *Leibstandarte*. En route it became embroiled in thick bitter fighting in a huge tank battle in the hills around Prokhorovka on 12 July. Here the Soviet 5th Guard and 5th Guard Tank Armies clashed with the powerful armoured *SS* units consequently resulting in the climax of operation '*Zitadelle*'. Throughout the attack the professionalism and technical ability of the *SS* was second to none. During the heavy fighting *SS* troops were often able to turn the balance even when the Russians had overwhelming superiority in numbers. In spite of the losses the units were imbued with optimism and continued to deliver to the enemy heavy blows.

During the climax of the battle both the 'Totenkopf' and 'Leibstandarte' attacked, whilst 'Das Reich' remained on the defensive, repelling a number of armour and infantry attacks. Although Russian losses in both men and equipment far exceeded the German, their losses could be replaced. German losses, however, except where armour could be recovered, were total. Within less than a week of Zitadelle being unleashed both sides had lost several hundred tanks and thousands of troops. While the Red Army was able to repair and replace its losses, the SS divisions had to struggle on with what they had left at their disposal. Constantly, the soldiers were being slowly ground down in a battle of attrition. The Russians had committed no less than seven corps, with more than 850 tanks and SU-85 assault guns. Wave upon wave of Russian T-34 tanks poured a storm of fire onto the SS positions. When the Soviet tanks ran out of ammunition, the crews often physically rammed the German tanks. Dismounted tanks crews then set about destroying the Panzers on foot using all weapons at their disposal, including grenades and mines.

Heavy battles of attrition were fought along many parts of the front, but it was the elite Waffen-SS soldiers that were taking the brunt of the fighting. Everywhere enemy troops charged Wehrmacht and SS positions, turning these once mighty soldiers from attackers to desperate defenders. Whole German regiments had no sooner attacked and captured an important position, when it was repeatedly

A Waffen-SS radio man during Kursk. By 7 July the advance of the SS.Panzer-Koprs seemed more promising than ever. Totenkopf had managed to smash its way through more than 30 miles of Russian line, whilst the Leibstandarte and Das Reich were equally successful despite enduring bitter fighting.

struck by waves of Russian tanks and mounted infantry and compelled to go over to the defensive.

By 13 July, the Germans were unable to make any further progress, and poor ground conditions were hampering its re-supply efforts. As a consequence Russian forces managed to drive back the 3.Panzer- Division in the area of the Rakovo-Kruglik road and recaptured hill 247, and the town of Berezovka. The following day, 'Totenkopf' was forced out of its bridgehead on the northern bank of the Psel River, while further east 'Das Reich' had made limited progress, capturing the town of Belenichino. The 'Grossdeutschland' Division was ordered to attack westwards, in order to recapture the ground lost by the 3.Panzer Division. Following another day of bitter fighting the division finally managed to link up with 3.Panzer at Berezovka, but it was unable to dislodge Russian forces from Hill 247.

On 15 July, 'Das Reich' made contact with the 7.Panzer-Division. However the Russian offensive to the north of the salient was now threatening the 9.Armee rear and it was forced to begin a planned withdrawal westwards to avoid encirclement. Following its withdrawal, almost all-offensive action around Prokhorovka ceased and German forces in the area went over to the defensive.

By 17 July, a further series of Russian offensives opened along the entire Eastern Front. The II.SS.Panzer-Korps and the 'Grossdeutschland' Division were withdrawn from 4. Panzer-Army, and the operation cancelled. By 23 July the 4.Panzer-Army had withdrawn to its start line.

Operation Zitadelle was a catastrophe for the German forces on the Eastern Front. Hitler had chosen an objective that was far too ambitious. The attack had also been continually delayed, allowing Russian forces additional time to prepare their defensive positions in the salient. Despite German efforts to batter their way through, they had neither the strength nor resources to do so. The cream of the

A Waffen-SS soldier can be seen in a four wheeled armoured car during a reconnaissance mission along the front lines. Within a few days of the battle reports confirmed that given the amount of Soviet prisoners taken and the damage inflicted on their lines, it appeared that the SS was poised on the edge of victory.

An SS soldier armed with a stick grenade moves forward during an attack against a Russian position. The initial phase of the fighting at Kursk had been very costly to the Russians, but in a tactical and operational sense it achieved its objectives. During the days that followed the Red Army began to deprive the SS of even tactical superiority.

German panzer force, so carefully concentrated prior to the operation, was exhausted and the Russian's had undeniably gained the initiative in the East. The campaign in Russia would now consist of a series of German withdrawals with the *Wehrmacht* and *Waffen-SS* fanatically contesting every foot of the way.

Many German commanders openly blamed the second front in Italy for draining German forces on the Eastern Front, and believed that they failed when Kursk was within their grasp. However, it is true that the second front did drain vital resources from Russia, but it would not have markedly improved its chances even if the second front had not begun, especially against an enemy of unrivalled strength. The Soviets at Kursk had undoubtedly delivered the *Wehrmacht* and *Waffen-SS* divisions a severe battering from which the German war effort was never to recover. The Germans had lost some thirty divisions, including seven Panzer divisions. According to official Soviet sources, as many as 49,822 German troops were killed or missing and had lost 1,614 tanks and self-propelled guns that were committed to action. As for the *SS* divisions, the '*Leibstandarte*', '*Das Reich*' and '*Totenkopf*' had lost more than half its vehicles and taken massive casualties. Red Army troops, however, suffered much higher losses with some 177,847 being killed and injured. They also lost a staggering 2,586 tanks and self-propelled guns during the battle.

Operation '*Zitadelle*' had finally ended the myth of the German invincibility and was the first time that the *blitzkrieg* concept had failed. The tide of victory in the East had finally been turned. But even as '*Zitadelle*' was drawing to a bloody conclusion, the *II.SS.Panzer-Korps* was not there to see the end of the battle: the remnants of their exhausted and battered units had already been hurriedly ordered to pull out of the Kursk area to the relative calm and quiet of Kharkov to wait for new orders. Before the *Leibstandarte* departed for Italy it turned over all of its remaining armoured fighting vehicles to 'Das Reich'. Both 'Totenkopf' and 'Das Reich' were detached from the 'Leibstandarte' and redeployed in the Donetz Basin on 25 July 1943. As for the 'Leibstandarte', the division was withdrawn on 3 August. A strong, tough and reliable SS division had been needed in Italy to prevent the whole peninsula from falling into Allied hands. For the next three months the 'Leibstandarte' spent its duration as Occupation Forces engaging periodically in anti-partisan operations in northern Italy and in Slovenia.

On the Eastern Front, the fighting had intensified. The Russians were determined not to allow the Germans any respite and launched a massive attack, overrunning *Feldmarschall* von Manstein's positions on the River Mius. Both 'Totenkopf' and 'Das Reich' were rushed north to protect Manstein's left flank.

A heavy MG42 machine gun position. The battle of the Kursk was probably the first modern Soviet operation of the war. Despite the fact that the Red Army lacked the technological superiority of individual weapons, they had a well-prepared defensive programme, which included elaborate deception plans to confuse the enemy.

SS troops converse with their commander during a pause in the heavy fighting at Kursk. Within days of the battle the Red Army had managed to ground down many of the SS units including those of the Wehrmacht as well.

A Wehrmacht anti-tank unit belonging to the 9th Army with their well camouflaged PaK38. All over the German northern front troops tried their best to push forward under relentless Russian fire. To the German soldier in this battle, it was unlike any other engagement they had previously encountered.

At Kursk Waffen-SS troops converse with their commander. Within days of the attack the Russians had managed to throw its offensive timetable completely off schedule. It was here on the blood soaked plains at Kursk that for the first time in the war the Red Army had savagely contested every foot of ground and was finally on an equal footing.

SS troops wearing their familiar SS camouflage smocks watch the battle unfolding across a field. Throughout the Kursk offensive the professionalism and technical ability of the SS was second to none.

Three photographs showing Waffen-SS MG42 machine gunners in one of the many trenches that littered the battlefield at Kursk. Through sheer weight of Soviet strength and stubborn combat along an ever-extending front, the German mobile units were finally being forced to a standstill as a result both SS and Wehrmacht troops used trenches to mount various attacks.

A heavy Wehrmacht MG42 machine gun position during intensive fighting against stubborn Russian resistance. In front of the German Army at Kursk stood six major defensive belts, each of which were subdivided into two or even three layers of almost impregnable strongholds.

A Waffen-SS machine gun crew with their MG34 machine gun. The primary gunner was known as the Schütze 1, whilst his team mate, Schütze 2, fed the ammunition belts and saw that the gun remained operational at all times.

A close-up view of an MG34 machine gunner using the optical sight provided with heavy machine guns. All three soldiers wear camouflaged canvas helmet covers, which were widely used by the Wehrmacht during this period of the war during the summer months.

Riflemen prepare to move forward into action. Within five days of heavy fighting many German units had lost immeasurable amounts of men and material. After a week of the attack the German Army had moved some 8-miles.

Four photographs showing an 8cm sGrW 34 mortar in action against an enemy target. Each battalion fielded some six of these excellent 8cm sGrW 34 mortars, which could fire 15 bombs per minute to a range of 2,625 yards. Aside from high-explosive and smoke bombs, this weapon also fired a "bounding" bomb. It was very common for infantry, especially during intensive long periods of action, to fire their mortar from either trenches or dug-in positions where the mortar crew could also be protected from enemy fire.

Three infantryman sit beside what is more than likely a captured Soviet shelter during. The Germans built very similar shelters too, which were called *Halbgruppenunterstande* (group and half-group living bunkers). These were to become essential for the *Landser* if they were to survive the ceaseless artillery and later the terrible freezing weather conditions.

A camouflaged battery of 15cm heavy field howitzers in a field. One of the howitzers is in a fixed position and its two steel wheels have been removed by the crew. The artillery bombardment that opened up the German offensive at Kursk was massive. After it subsided infantry and armour poured forward with artillery units following in the wake of the forward spearheads.

An anti-tank crew during a lull in the fighting. In the 9th Army, XIII Army Korps was by far the strongest Korps in both men and anti-tank guns. It faced the strongest defensive positions in the entire salient and was used as a battering ram against the strong Russian defensive positions.

An MG42 light machine gun position. Although a machine gun troop was normally a three man squad, due to the high casualty rates suffered on the Eastern Front they were commonly reduced to just two, but still highly effective.

Two photographs showing the 15cm Nebelwerfer 41 being prepared for firing and launching the deadly six-barrelled rocket launcher into action. This weapon fired 2.5kg shells that could be projected over a range of 7,000 metres. When fired the projectiles screamed through the air, causing the enemy to become unnerved by the noise. These fearsome weapons that caused extensive carnage at Kursk served in independent army rocket launcher battalions, and later in the war in regiments and brigades.

A soldier on look-out during a lull in the fighting with his well dug-in 8cm sGrW 34 mortar. It was very common for infantry, especially during intensive long periods of action, to fire their mortar from either trenches or dug-in positions where the mortar crew could also be protected from enemy fire.

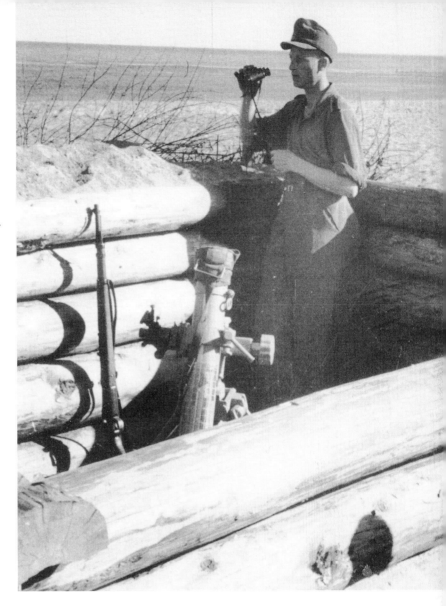

Wehrmacht troops are in the process of digging a defensive position. Slowly and systematically the Red Army began to pulverise the German lines into the ground prompting many units to go onto the defensive and dig trenches and other forms of defensive positions to stay alive.

Two photographs showing the gun crew of a modified 10.5cm le FH 18/42, preparing to fire the gun in anger. The 10.5cm was the standard light artillery piece deployed in the artillery divisions on the Eastern Front. However, in order to give the gun better punch on the battlefield the weapon was modified in 1942. The barrel was lengthened, a cage muzzlebrake was fitted, and the carriage was a lightened version of the le FH 18 design.

Infantry of the Das Reich Division advance along a road passing a burning building. During the first days of Kursk Das Reich had made exceedingly good progress and infiltrated enemy lines in front of them.

A Waffen-SS Sd.Kfz.251 halftrack armed with a 7.5cm short gun barrel of a Pz.Kpfw.IV during operations at Kursk in July 1943. Note the white painted kill rings on the barrel of the 7.5cm gun.

Two members of an MG42 prepare to open fire on suspected enemy targets. This light MG is being used from its bipod mount. With the bipod extended and the belt loaded, the machine gunner could effectively move the weapon quickly from one position to another and throw it to the ground and put it into operation, with deadly effect.

The MG42 had tremendous staying power against enemy infantry and during the last two years of the war soldiers took to continuously deploying their machine guns in the most advantageous defensive positions.

Two photographs showing a s.IG33 infantry gun from an SS regiment's infantry gun company being used against an enemy target. Much of the infantry regiments used on the Eastern Front were horse mounted and these heavy guns were almost invariably brought to the front by horse drawn transport.

A Waffen-SS crew have utilised their 8.8cm Flak gun against a ground target during heavy fighting. By 1943 the deadly 8.8cm Flak gun was used extensively both against ground and aerial targets.

A projectile is being placed inside the 5cm barrel of the leGrW36 mortar. The leGrW36 intended role was to engage pockets of resistance that were beyond the range of hand grenades. It was designed for high angled fire only (no less than 42°). The main drawbacks of the weapon were its inadequate range and the limited effectiveness of its ammunition, which were regarded as not heavy enough.

An MG34 machine gunner with ammunition feeder during the Kursk offensive. The MG34 machine gun was one of the most popular weapons used both in the Wehrmacht and Waffen-SS. It had tremendous defensive staying power against enemy infantry during the last two years of the war.

A common scene during the later stages of the Kursk offensive. Here Waffen-SS infantry have been driven from their positions and take cover along an embankment filled with mud and water.

Waffen-SS troops marching towards the front lines against growing enemy resistance. In spite of the heavy losses the units were imbued with optimism and continued to deliver the enemy heavy blows.

Here in this photograph a Waffen-SS MG34 machine gunner can be seen concealed in undergrowth with his weapon. The machine gun has the MG34 50-round basket drum magazine fitted.

Two photographs showing a Waffen-SS with their PaK gun. At Kursk the Russians had committed no less than seven corps, with more than 850 tanks and SU-85 assault guns. Wave upon wave of Russian T-34 tanks poured a storm of fire on to both SS and Wehrmacht positions.

In a field is a heavy MG34 machine gun. The MG34 is mounted on a sustained fire-mount. In every infantry battalion there fielded eight MG34 heavy machine guns on the sustained-fire mount, which was regarded in 1943, more than enough to keep open the flanks for attacking infantry.

SS troops press their Schwimmwagen amphibious car across a river during operations at Kursk. A motorcycle and its rider have been precariously positioned on the rear of the four-wheeled vehicle whilst the driver and his mate can been seen navigating the crossing.

Two photographs showing the MG34 heavy machine gun, one being transported by a schwimmwagen amphibious car still on the sustained-fire mount, whilst the other in action in a fixed position. Each infantry battalion contained an MG Kompanie, which fielded eight MG34 heavy machine-guns on the sustained-fire mount.

Five photographs showing the 8cm sGrW 34 mortar being loaded and fired in anger against an enemy target. Note how all the crew duck for cover to avoid the back blast as the projectile leaves the gun tube. Two of the ammunition handlers or loaders can be seen holding the tripod in order to keep it steady and accurate when firing. This mortar earned a deadly reputation in line on the Eastern Front and captured 34s were eagerly employed against the Germans.

Chapter Two

Fighting Withdrawal

As the winter of 1943 approached, a feeling of despair and gloom gripped the German front lines. To many of the soldiers there was a dull conviction that the war was lost, and yet there was still no sight of its end. Being always outnumbered, perpetually short of fuel and ammunition, and having to constantly exert themselves and their machinery to the very limits of endurance had a profound effect on life at the front. During the later half of 1943 the equipment situation continued to deteriorate, especially in the Panzer units. The effect

Army Group South and an 8.8cm FlaK crew are seen here connecting the guns limber for transportation following the failure at Kursk in mid July 1943. By the end of July Army Group South had a total of 822,000 troops opposing an estimated 1,710,000 Soviet troops.

An SS crew of a Schimmwagen amphibious car smile for the camera. In front of them in a field are an Sd.Kfz.251 halftrack and a stationary Panther V tank. For the Waffen-SS and Wehrmacht the Eastern Front summer campaign had been completely disastrous.

Waffen-SS radio men with their Torn. Fu. B1 S/E radio pack during the summer of 1943. These widely used portable radios were carried by a soldier on a specially designed back-pack frame, and when connected to each other (upper and lower valves) via special cables, could be used on the march.

Another photograph showing a Panther V tank from the same regiment in a wheat field during operations on the Eastern Front in the summer of 1943. During Kursk the Panther saw its operational debut, but during the battle many of them experienced mechanical failure and other problems.

A typical scene after a heavy down pour of rain on the Eastern Front. Here SS troops including a Panzer crewman lend a hand to try and relieve a motorcycle combination from sinking further into the mire.

Waffen-SS anti-tank gunners in a field have extensively camouflaged their PaK gun with heavy foliage during operations on the Russian central front in the late summer of 1943. The PaK gun provided both the Waffen-SS and Wehrmacht with not only effective fire support but also defensive staying power as troops found themselves confronted everywhere by increasing numbers of enemy tanks.

of starving the experienced and elite formations like the *Waffen-SS* was a constant concern for the tacticians. The *SS* did receive a high proportion of tanks, artillery and assault guns, but this was in stark contrast to the enormous volume of armaments being produced by the Russians. The *SS* were thus faced with a dangerous and worsening prospect, but unlike the normal German soldier many of these elite troops retained their fanatical determination on the battlefield. Against the growing Soviet 'menace' they still proved to be first class formations. Their new role as the so-called 'fire brigades', being shuttled from one danger spot to another to dampen down heavy Russian attacks, typified their position during late 1943. In total there were seven SS divisions that became Hitler's emergency 'fire brigade', and it was in October 1943 that these seven crack SS.Panzergrenadier Divisions – 'Leibstandarte Adolf Hitler', 'Das Reich', 'Totenkopf', 'Wiking', 'Hohenstaufen', 'Frundsberg', and 'Hitlerjugend' – were redesignated SS Panzer divisions.

The seven new divisions maintained and enhanced the military reputation of the *Waffen-SS*. As the *Wehrmacht* established defensive lines in the face of the advancing enemy, commanders looked at the aggressive and loyal striking force of the *SS* to be counted upon to snatch victory from defeat. It was for this reason that Hitler was forced to order the return of the 'Leibstandarte' from Italy. By November 1943, barely three months after departing, the division now completely rested, and re-equipped with the latest tanks and assault guns returned to its old fighting ground in the East.

The *SS* division arrived on the battlefield south of Kiev in early November 1943. It was to be the main attacking division in the 4.Panzer-Division and was to strike northwards towards Kiev, which had already fallen into enemy hands.

In other areas of the Eastern Front German units fought well with distinction to contain the Russians from marching across the western Ukraine. However, the unrelenting fighting had proven to be more costly. As the winter of 1943 reared its head during October, a feeling of further despair and gloom prevailed across the entire German Army. To the depressed soldiers that had to endure the third Russia winter a dull conviction gripped them that the war in the East was not lost – yet without any sight of its end. Both the German Army and Waffen-SS were still dug deep in to the heartlands of the Soviet Union. But unlike 1941 and 1942, they had lost the initiative. Slowly and defiantly the German soldier retreated back across a bleak and hostile landscape, always outnumbered, constantly low on fuel, ammunition and other desperate supplies. In three months following the defeat at Kursk Army Group South alone had only received some 32,000 replacements, although it suffered more than 130,000 casualties. The equipment situation too continued to decline, especially in Panzer units. The whole German Army in the East was thus faced with a dangerous and worsening prospect than ever before.

A well dug-in 5cm PaK 38 during the early autumn of 1943. The PaK 38 was the first anti-tank weapon to be produced as full-sized artillery. Although these anti-tank guns proved deadly during the earlier part of the war, German gunners soon realised that they required something more potent to counter the growing menace of Soviet armour.

To make matters worse, an anti-partisan conflict added yet another dimension to the war in Russia. With word of the advancing Red Army, Ukrainian nationalist partisans, Polish underground groups and communist partisans began raiding German outposts, barracks, police stations, rail depots, supply dumps, ambushing convoys and trains. As the German troops withdrew they had to clear out the partisans before they became prey to the snipers and saboteurs. All this and continuous pressure from Hitler to defend every yard of land with their blood, made fighting even more inhumane. For the German Army and Waffen-SS the approaching winter passed like the summer and autumn, in a sequence of bitter bloodthirsty battles, which consequently sapped the will and energy of the German strength almost beyond repair.

Troops with the standard 15cm Nebelwerfer 41. Because it was dangerous for the crew to remain close to the launcher while the piece was being fired, it was fired remotely using an electrical detonator attached to a cable, which ran to the piece.

Waffen-SS troops with a Nebelwerfer during a lull in the fighting. The electrical cable that led to the remote firing mechanism can be just seen running from the gun tube between the two wheels. The Nebelwerfer was mounted on the same carriage as that of the 3.7cm PaK35/36.

Waffen-SS troops pose for the camera in front of an Sd.Kfz.251 armoured personnel carrier. As the winter of 1943/44 reared its head during October, a feeling of further despair and gloom prevailed across the Eastern Front.

A Waffen-SS soldier wearing a winter reversible uniform in a fortified position in order to afford some protection from enemy fire. The MG34 machine gunner is firing on long range targets using the optical sight provided to heavy machine-guns.

Waffen-SS troops in northern Russia are erecting a wooden shelter in preparation for the harsh winter conditions that are fast approaching in October 1943.

An SS mortar crew in action in some wooded area. Although the SS were slowly being driven further west by overwhelming enemy superiority they were still fighting with fanatical determination on the battlefield.

A photograph taken the moment a Wespe fires a projectile from its 10.5cm le.FH 18/2 L/28 gun. The crew inside the vehicle are protected by a light armoured superstructure mounted on a chassis of a Pz.Kpfw.II. The vehicle served in armoured artillery battalions but were lightly armoured, and as a result many of them were lost in battle.

A Pz.Kpfw.IV passes a halftrack during operations in southern Russia during the last months of 1943. After the German defeat at Kursk, Army Group tried its best to hold onto vital areas of ground in order to contain the overly extended front.

During the night a 15cm heavy field howitzer opens fire on a Russian target. As the projectile leaves the barrel it generates a massive flash that lights up the night sky.

An MG34 heavy machine gun team move forward into action. The term light and heavy machine guns defined the role and not the weight of the gun. This machine gun is being fired from a sustained fire-mount.

The crew of a 10.5cm heavy field howitzer are in a field during a lull in the fighting and waiting for the order to resume firing again. Ammunition can be stacked in special crates. Note the guns aiming stake is being temporarily used as a tent pole.

Well camouflaged infantry in a forest clearing. They are wearing their waterproof zeitbahn to protect themselves from the harsh elements. Note that foliage has been attached to their steel helmets,

SS officers relax in a field during a lull in the fighting. Slowly the Waffen-SS and their Wehrmacht counterparts were being pushed back across a bleak and hostile landscape, always outnumbered, constantly low on fuel, ammunition and other desperate supplies.

Six photographs showing mortar crews in action during the last months of 1943. A mortar crew usually consisted of at least three members. The gunner controlled the deflection and elevation of the weapon. The assistant gunner loaded the round at the command of the gunner. The ammunition man prepared and handed over ammunition to the assistant gunner. One of the most impressive mortars used by the Germans on the Eastern Front was the 12cm Granatwerfer 378(r). The weapon consisted of a circular base plate, the tube and the supporting bipod, weighing 285kg. Because of its excessive weight, a two wheeled axle was utilised, enabling the mortar to be towed into action. The axle could then be quickly removed before firing. The weapon fired the Wurfgranate 42 round, which carried 3.1kg of explosives.

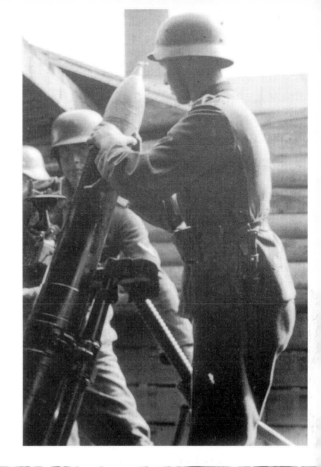

A number of Wehrmacht troops plug their ears as the 15cm field howitzer is about to be fired. Note the trail spades dug into the ground. These were designed to help prevent the full impact of the howitzer's recoil after firing and reduce the backward movement of the gun.

A photograph showing a heavy MG42 machine gun position on a sustained-fire mount. In open terrain the MG42 machine gun squad would use their sustained fire-mount to protect the flanks of advancing rifle companies. However, in built-up areas the crews often had to operate forward with the rifle platoons and in light machine gun roles with bipods only. They were able to still sometimes take advantage of the situation and revert back to a heavy machine gun role.

A group of soldiers on a specially designed flatbed railway car pose for the camera with their tracked vehicle. Even during the Wehrmacht's retreat it was common for entire divisions to move its men and equipment by rail. This saved the division considerable time and wear and tear on its machines.

A soldier in a defensive position with his heavy MG42 machine gun. Throughout the last months of 1943 the German Army was compelled to fight and defend its position to the bitter end. In spite of the mounting casualties Hitler still prohibited all voluntary withdrawals.

A PaK crew rest with their weapon in late 1943. One of the most important defensive and offensive tactics for the Wehrmacht during the war, especially on the Eastern Front, was its ability to counter enemy armour on the battlefield. By 1943 as the Red Army increased its tank strength the Germans were needing more potent anti-tank guns that would be required on the battlefield to help prevent the growing might of the Russian tanks and its thick armour.

One of the quickest forms of transportation across the vast expanses of Russia was on bicycle. Here in this photograph SS infantry have dismounted from their bicycles. Their personal kit can be seen attached to the handle-bars. They all appear to be armed with the Mauser bolt action rifle.

Leibstandarte troops south of Kiev in November 1943. By November barely three months after departing, the Leibstandarte now completely rested, and re-equipped with the latest tanks and assault guns returned to its old fighting ground in the East.

An SS artillery crew rest. A halftrack prime mover can be seen towing a camouflaged 15cm s.IG33 gun. This particular infantry gun was a reliable and robust weapon and was used extensively by the Waffen-SS until the end of the war.

An SS light MG34 machine gunner. In this photograph, the MG34 is about to fire his weapon on the bipod. Rifle groups generally had a light machine-gun with a bipod, along with one or two spare barrels. A heavy machine-gun group, however, had the bipod fitted machine gun, but additionally carried a tripod with optical sight.

An SS artillery crew during a contact with an enemy position with their 7.5cm le.IG 18 artillery gun. This weapon could not only be fired quickly and accurately but also had an advantage on the battlefield by having a low profile design and splinter shield.

Waffen-SS troops move a long a slit trench during operations somewhere on the Eastern Front in late 1943. By this period casualties were rising dramatically in the ranks of both the Wehrmacht and Waffen-SS with limited reserves to replace the high losses.

A Waffen-SS heavy mortar team move through a forest somewhere in central Russia during the early autumn of 1943. Note that each man wears the camouflage smock commonly associated with SS troops.

A Waffen-SS MG42 machine gunner and his team advance a long a typical muddy road in late 1943. When times and conditions allowed, machine gun crews invariably prepared a number of fall-back positions. They appreciated the full value of the MG42, and along these fall-back positions the machine gunners were able to set-up advantageous defensive positions.

During a lull in the fighting a group of Waffen-SS soldiers of the Totenkopf-Division cook some much needed food over a fire. This photograph was taken near Krivoi Rog where the SS division were attempting to hold vital ground against strong Russian forces.

Two SS soldiers joke during operations in the East. Although after the battle of the Kursk the Waffen-SS never regained the strength it once possessed, it had received more replacements in both men and equipment.

SS infantry carry a six-metre medium pneumatic boat. A number of heavy pieces of equipment could also be loaded on these boats, which included the 8cm mortar, 2cm anti-aircraft gun and 7.5cm infantry gun.

Troops, most of which are posing for the camera in their new winter reversible parkas which are being worn grey side out.

Two Totenkopf officers converse with a soldier armed with a Mauser bolt action rifle in late 1943. During this period the Totenkopf-Division dug-in near Krivoi Rog and prepared its units for another Russian assault.

SS artillerymen can be seen in a field with a 7.5cm le IG light artillery gun. This weapon was one of the first post World War One guns to be issued to the Wehrmacht and later the SS. The gun was light and robust and employed a shotgun breech action.

Two photographs showing Waffen-SS and Wehrmacht mortar crews with the standard German mortar was the 8cm Granatwerfer 34 or Gr.W.34 mortar. The mortars maximum range was 2.4km when it fired the standard Wurfgranate 34 round which carried 550g of explosives. The round could be set to detonate on impact or in an airburst. It could also fire the Wurfgranate 40, a larger round with an increased explosive charge of almost 5kg. However this decreased the maximum range to 950m.

Wehrmacht troops armed with rifles and a flamethrower storm a burning Russian position during intensive fighting. The battles that continued until the end of 1943 clearly demonstrated that the Red Army was rapidly developing into a skilful army with enormous quantities of men and material.

A photograph taken the moment a 10.5cm artillery crew fire at an enemy position. Various pieces of foliage have been covered over the trail spades and part of the splinter shield and wheels in order try and conceal the weapon from aerial observation.

In a forward observation post a Waffen-SS officer can be seen standing next to a pair of scissor binoculars. From this position the men could send through details of enemy movements back to divisional headquarters.

A group of SS troops rest during the late winter of 1943. By this stage of the war the SS and their Wehrmacht counterparts were not only fighting against numerically superior enemy forces but increased partisan activity as well to the rear of the main lines.

Two photographs showing the Wehrmacht and Waffen-SS waiting for orders to fire their 10.5cm heavy field howitzer. Even during the withdrawal in the second half of 1943 combat experience soon showed that artillery support was of decisive importance in both defensive and offensive roles.

A heavy MG34 machine gun crew with their commanding officer. The MG34 has been attached to a Lafette 34 sustained-fire mount with optical sight. The MG34 had tremendous staying power on the battlefield, and a well-deployed, well-supplied gun crew could easily hold a large area for some considerable time.

Three Waffen-SS soldiers pose for the camera in a trench after receipt of their decorations earned for bravery in combat during the fighting in late 1943.

Chapter Three

Winter Warfare

The military situation on the Eastern Front in January 1944 was dire for the German Army. It had entered the New Year with a dwindling number of soldiers to man the battle lines. The Red Army, however, was now even in greater strength than ever before and Hitler's reluctance to concede territory was still proving to be very problematic for commanders in the field. The persistent lack of strategic decision in the East was causing major trouble too. Nevertheless, in spite of the worsening condition of the German Army, the soldiers were compelled to fight on.

In Army Group North, General George Kuechler's force had been for some weeks trying in vain to hold its positions along its northern defences against strong Russia forces. From the Volkhov River to the Gulf of Finland the front was covered with a string of trenches and shell holes, reminiscent of trench warfare during World War One. By 15 January 1944, the defences were finally attacked by three powerful Soviet fronts, the Leningrad, Volkhov and Second Baltic. The 18th Army, which bore the brunt of the main attacks, were outnumbered by at least 3:1 in divisions. As usual German troops were expected to hold the front, but over-whelming enemy fire power proved too much for Kuechler's Army Group and

In a defensive position and a machine gunner can be seen standing next to a MG34 heavy machine gun on the sustained-fire mount. Each infantry battalion contained an MG company, which fielded eight MG34 heavy machine-guns on the sustained-fire mount.

Luftwaffe field division troops rest wearing the winter reversible smock white-side out. Initially on the Eastern Front the Luftwaffe field divisions were simply thrown into combat without proper training or leadership. However, by early 1944 the army finally took full command of these formations.

was compelled to fall back under a hurricane of enemy fire. Within four days of the attack the Russians had successfully breached Army Group North's defences in three places. This effectively wrenched open a huge corridor allowing the Red Army to pour through towards the besieged city of Leningrad. Troops of the German 18th Army were beginning to disintegrate. Already it had incurred 40,000 casualties trying to contain the Soviets. Fighting in the mud and freezing water, the men were totally exhausted and unable to hold back the enemy for any appreciable length of time. Hitler on the other hand still prohibited all voluntary withdrawals and reserved all decisions to withdraw himself. In a leadership conference held by the *Führer* the commanders were told to infuse determination in their men and to strengthen faith in ultimate victory. But in spite of Hitler's radical measures in trying to generate the will to fight until success was secured, the German Army were unable to stem the rout of the advancing Russian forces.

By 26 January the city of Leningrad was liberated after nine hundred days of siege. The 18th Army was now split into three parts and struggled to hold any

Anti-tank gunners with their lethal white washed 5cm PaK 38 out in the snow in January 1944. The PaK 38 was well liked among the crews that had the chance to use it in battle. Not only was the weapon effective in combat, but also easy to conceal.

type of front forward of the Luga River. The entire German Northern Front was now beginning to crumble and Hitler openly blamed Kuechler for its failure. On 1 February 1944 the General was relieved of his command and temporarily replaced by Hitler's Eastern Front 'trouble shooter', General Walther Model. Model was a great improviser who was quite capable of changing the tactical situation in Army Group North. Almost immediately Model went to work by introducing his 'Schild und Schwert' (Shield and Sword) policy, which stated that no soldiers were to withdraw without express permission, only if it paved the way for a counterstroke later. Along the front both the 16th and 18th Armies, which were badly depleted with only the 12th Panzer and 58th Infantry Divisions intact were ordered to hold the line on the Luga River, east of a series of heavily constructed defences known as the Panther Line. Model, determined at all costs to prevent the front degenerating into a panic flight collected stragglers and sent them back to the line. He cancelled leaves, sent walking wounded to their units, and sent a number of the rear-echelon troops to the front. Without hesitation he requested more reinforcements, which included Waffen-SS replacements, naval coastal batteries and Luftwaffe troops.

Throughout February moral was temporarily restored to the front line units as the German forces stepped back to defend the Panther Line they had slightly gained enough strength to hold back the Red Army. During March the Russians began exerting more pressure, especially against the 16th Army that was defending positions along the Baltic. But the spring thaw had arrived early and melting snow had turned the roads on which the Russians were travelling into a quagmire. The conditions were so bad that forward units from the 16th Army reported that Soviet tanks could be seen sinking up to their turrets in mud. It seemed the Panther Line was holding, with the weather playing a major part in containing the Red Army. Now it would not be until the early summer that the Red Army would resume its push. Thanks to Model, Army Group North was now established. Due to his

A soldier appears to be trying to fix a part broken on a cart. By January 1944, the military situation on the Eastern Front was dire for the German Army. It had entered the New Year with dwindling numbers of soldiers to man the already over extended battle lines.

Wehrmacht troops pose for the camera in a dug out in the early winter of 1944. The soldier's lack of winter clothing indicates the problems of supply in some areas of the front, even by this period of the war.

A mortar crew with their well dug-in 8cm sGrW 34 mortar. Life in the line for these soldiers was a continuous grind. There was little respite – if the Red Army let up for a brief period, the sub zero temperatures certainly did not.

It shows a Waffen-SS machine gun crew going on the offensive with an MG34 machine gun mounted on a Dreifuss 34 anti-aircraft tripod mount. One of the most important factors in overwhelming the enemy was when Soviet forces faced a well supplied machine gun team with plenty of ammunition.

energetic, innovative and courageous method of leadership he had prevented the wholesale collapse of the northern sector of the Eastern Front.

Model's success in the north now earned him a new command in Army Group South. On 30 March 1944, less than a week before Army Group South was re-designated Army Group North Ukraine, Model replaced Manstein and was installed as Commander-in-Chief.

For three long months Army Group South had fought a series of bitter and bloody battles in order to stem the gradual deterioration of its forces in southern Russia. Conditions for the Germany Army and the Waffen-SS between January and March 1944 were dismal. Supplies were inadequate, and replacements in men were far below what was needed to sustain its divisions along the entire front. To make matters worse in early January a 110-mile breach between Army Group Centre and Army Group South had developed. Neither army group had sufficient forces to plug the gap and by the end of the month the gap opened even wider when the Belorussian Front pushed the 2nd Army to the lone of the Ipa River.

For the next few weeks further pressure was applied on Army Group South. By this time the German front was disintegrating under persistent overwhelming enemy attacks. German mobile reserves had all been worn down to almost extinction and this led to a number of units being encircled. One of the largest pockets to develop was in the Kovel-Korsun area of the lower Dnieper where seven German divisions and the premier 5th SS Wiking Division were trapped. By using some the last Panzers in the area, Manstein managed to drive a wedge and create a corridor for the encircled men and held it open to allow them to escape. The remnants of the shattered divisions that successfully broke out struggled south-east under continuous Russian fire.

A FlaK gunner protecting a position against aerial attack. The projectiles used for this weapon were airburst shells. The airburst shell was favoured for their anti-personnel capabilities against troops in cover.

A photograph taken during the early winter of 1944 showing a well camouflaged 10.5cm l.FH18M gun crew wearing various personal equipment prior to going into action. These light field howitzers were constantly modified during the war in order to increase their ranges.

To the north of Kovel-Korsun the situation of the rest of Manstein's Army Group was equally dire. The bulk of the men were totally exhausted. The worn out 1st and 4th Panzer armies were all that were left to support troop operations in the south, and they were being slowly compressed against the Carpathian Mountains. By early March advanced Soviet units had reached the outskirts of the city of Tarnopol. Within days of their arrival Red Army troops advanced through the ravaged city but were soon beaten back by strong German defences. As German soldiers fought for Tarnopol Hitler issued another order appealing for his forces on the Eastern Front to use towns and cities and surrounding areas as fortified positions in order to slow down the Soviet drive westward. In other words he was calling upon every soldier to hold to the last man. Many troops that were given this awesome task of defending the towns and cities nicknamed these suicidal assignments as *Himmelfahrts-Kommnandos* (missions to Heaven).

In the city of Tarnopol conditions for the troops were appalling. For days they

In Army Group North and Wehrmacht troops can be seen the front lines. For some weeks Army Group North had been trying in vain to hold positions along its northern defences against strong Russian forces.

held out inside the ruins whilst being subjected to a number of sustained bombardments from heavy Soviet artillery. By 21 March, the Red Army of the 1st and 4th Tank Armies smashed through the front swiftly carrying along with them like driftwood, remnants of the German defensive line consisting mainly of the 68th Infantry and 7th Panzer Divisions. Two days later the Russian 1st Tank Army wheeled west with all its might and hammered its way through bewildered German infantry divisions that were defending Tarnopol. Those troops that were defending surrounding areas were thrown back some ten miles, leaving behind a garrison inside the doomed city. Some of the defenders of Tarnopol reported that the scenes were reminiscent of Stalingrad. For the next three weeks the four thousand strong garrison held out. When a rescue mission by the 9th SS Division tried to relieve the trapped force only fifty-three men managed to break out during the night of April 15/16 and reach the German lines. The rest were captured or killed.

In spite the horrifying casualties and huge losses of equipment inflicted upon Army Group South, its forces as a whole during the winter of 1944 had generally defended its positions relatively well against terrible odds. In fact in some places it even held the line. When Model replaced Manstein at the end of March the crisis in the south was temporarily relieved as the Russian winter offensive gradually died away. The Red Army after nearly eight months of continuous movement had at last given respite to the Wehrmacht and Waffen-SS. However, unbeknown to Army Group South, the Russians were preparing for a massive attack against the German centre, which was to carry them to the banks of the River Vistula in Poland. The German Army was soon to be vanquished from the Soviet Union.

A soldier in a defensive position armed with an MP38/40 machine pistol. He is wearing a white washed steel helmet and a two-piece white camouflage smock and black leather boots.

From the same defensive position and German infantry can be seen inside the trench wearing two-piece snowsuits and their steel helmets have received an application of white wash for camouflage.

German troops withdraw westward following the capture of Leningrad on 26 January 1944. All the soldiers are wearing the two piece snow suit and armed with the Mauser bolt action rife.

Gebirgsjager troops fire a 7.5cm Geb36 gun. Firing an artillery piece in the snow could be frequently problematic for the gun crew. The recoil would regularly drive the weapon deep into the snow and would often cause inaccurate firing. For this reason this 7.5cm Geb36 gun has been modified – its wheels have been removed and replaced with sturdy gun trails.

A white washed 15cm s.FH18 heavy field howitzer is being readied for action. The 15cm field howitzer was designed to attack targets deeper into the enemy rear. This included command posts, reserve units, assembly areas, and logistic facilities. Note the stacked pile of wicker ammunition cases.

During a lull in the fighting and Wehrmacht troops can be seen cooking food over an open fire in the snow. During this period the Germans in Army Group North had managed to temporarily strengthen its defences in the region and hold back the Red Army.

Two soldier in a trench armed with Mauser riles and wearing white camouflage smocks. Although the white camouflage smock was a popular and practical item of winter clothing it tended to be worn night and day for weeks. Soon they became filthy, thus defeating the objective of the white camouflage.

A light MG42 machine gunner and crew in the snow during defensive actions in Army Group North. Although along many sectors of the front the Germans were successfully holding back the advancing Red Army, it came with a high price in men and materials.

A photograph taken the moment a 15cm s.IG.33 is fired in anger against enemy positions. Although the German soldier was capable of meeting the highest standards, fighting courageously with self-sacrifice against massive numerical superiority, he could only delay the enemy, not defeat them.

Two photographs taken in sequence during the winter of 1944 showing a 10.5cm light field howitzer in action against an enemy position. The 10.5cm light field howitzer was a very versatile weapon and was widely used by both the Wehrmacht and Waffen-SS until the end of the war. All German infantry divisions had field artillery regiments and these consisted of batteries that contained the 10.5cm l.FH18 light field howitzer. During this period of the war another 10.5cm l.FH18M was introduced. Unlike this model in the photograph it had a muzzle break to help mitigate against excessive recoilforces, which allowed heavier shells to be fired, increasing the guns range as well.

A mortar crew pose for the camera out in the snow during defensive actions in Army Group South in late January early February 1944.

Wehrmacht troops being supported by a StuG.III in the snow. The StuG.III had been a very popular assault gun on the battlefield. The vehicles had initially provided crucial mobile fire support to the infantry, and also proved their worth as invaluable anti-tank weapon. However, by the early winter of 1944 the StuG was primarily used as an anti-tank weapon, thus depriving the infantry of vital fire support.

Tracked and wheeled vehicles have halted on a road during the winter of 1944 towing anti-tank guns towards the front lines. An Sd.Kfz.2 or Kettenkrad can be seen trundling along the road carrying supplies and a soldier onboard.

Wearing Greatcoats and two piece camouflage smocks a 10.5cm heavy infantry gun crew are preparing their weapon for firing. The gun's projectiles can be seen stacked on wooden ammunition cases.

Two Wehrmacht soldiers wearing the two piece reversible winter camouflage suit white-side-out are sited inside dug-out both armed with the MP38/40 machine pistol. Two stick grenades can also be identified nearby.

Fighting in the extreme arctic conditions and a mortar crew inside a dug-out prepare to fire one of the projectiles against an enemy target.

Two photographs of Wehrmacht troops wearing white camouflage winter smocks preparing to use their PaK35/36 anti-tank gun. This weapon was the first anti-tank gun mass produced and saw service in both the Wehrmacht and Waffen-SS.

From a slit trench soldiers can be seen poised for action. The soldier nearest to the camera is armed with the Kar98 carbine bolt-action rifle which was the standard issue piece of weaponry supplied to the German Army throughout the war. Attached to his black leather belt is a P38 holster and bayonet for his rifle.

Two photographs showing soldiers wearing the revisible winter clothing. Apart from being extremely comfortable and warm, these uniforms provided the wearer with greater freedom of movement, especially with personal equipment.

Soldiers wearing white camouflage smocks inside a trench along the Panther Line in early February 1944. Both the German 16th and 18th Armies were ordered to hold the line on the Luga River, east of a series of heavily constructed defences known as the Panther Line.

A Waffen-SS soldier not wearing any white camouflage takes cover by lying in the snow during defensive operations somewhere on the Eastern Front.

The crew of a Hummel self-propelled gun wearing the reversible parka grey-side out have halted in a field with a battery of Hummel's during a defensive action in very early 1944. The Hummel mounted the standard 15cm heavy field howitzer in a lightly armoured fighting compartment built on the chassis of a Pz.Kpfw.III/IV.

Desperately required vehicles for the Eastern Front have arrived on special railroad flat cars and are being unloaded for delivery to the badly depleted forces. By this period of the war Panzer divisions required massive numbers of replacements, but because there were so many that needed replacing in the field the Panzer divisions were compelled to carry on regardless.

Two rather dirty and dishevelled Wehrmacht soldiers sit next to their shelter along the Panther Line in February 1944. Note the captured Soviet PPsH submachine gun piled next to other riles. This reliable weapon was very popular with the German soldiers until the end of the war.

 A photograph taken the moment a modified 10.5cm le FH 18/42 is fired against an enemy target during fighting in Army Group Centre in early 1944. The gun has received an application of winter white wash paint and blends well with the local terrain.

The crew of a PaK35/36 anti-tank gun prepare their gun for action. Due to the local terrain being a mix of snow, grass and mud, because of the thaw, two of the crew have taken to wearing their two piece camouflage suits grey-side-out.

A well camouflaged troop leader armed with a 9mm MP38/40 machine-pistol. The MP38/40 machine pistol was commonly called the "Schmeisser". He is also armed with a M1924 stick grenade and wears a pair of 6 x 30 field binoculars.

A 10.5cm infantry gun in action somewhere on the Eastern Front in early 1944. Throughout the war the 10.5cm gun provided both the Wehrmacht and Waffen-SS with a versatile, relatively mobile, base of fire.

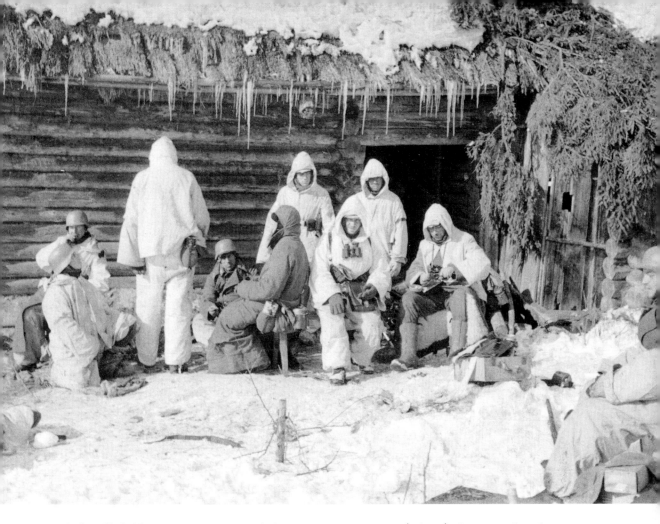

Luftwaffe field troops rest next to their temporary accommodation during operations in early 1944. By late 1943 Luftwaffe field divisions strength on the Eastern Front varied from 6,000–16,000. Most had to make do with second-rate weaponry or captured equipment.

A halftrack tows an 8.8cm FlaK gun towards the front lines in early 1944. Losses suffered in the continuous battles of early 1944 would further weaken and reduce the effectiveness of the German Army. Time was now running out.

Infantryman sit beside a shelter during operations in early 1944. The shelters which the Germans built were called *Halbgruppenunterstande* (group and half-group living bunkers). These were to become essential for the *Landser* if they were to survive the ceaseless artillery and terrible freezing weather conditions.

A light MG34 machine gunner lying near the entrance of his dug-out. By this period of the war the East German infantry divisions had been severely mauled. A number had suffered serious losses, but could still be re-equipped without withdrawing them completely from combat.

Well concealed inside a wooded area the crew of white-washed 7.5cm PaK40 can be seen with their deadly anti-tank weapon. The PaK40 had spaced-armour shield which was held together by large bolts. These bolts also had drilled holed that allowed the crews to thread foliage through them.

Three Wehrmacht troops rest next to a deserted building in early 1944. The troop leader on the right is armed with an MP38/40 machine-pistol, whilst his comrades are equipped with the Kar98K bolt action rifle.

A light MG42 machine gun crew out in a field. The train of view for the gunner must have been immense and would have certainly offered a very good opportunity for detecting enemy movement from some distance away.

On the front line and Waffen-SS troops tuck into their rations. Rations among these soldiers seem plentiful with loaves of bread and various tins of rations spread along the trench. Within months food supplies to the front lines had severely diminished making life for the soldier very difficult.

A mortar crew prepare their weapon for action in the snow. The Germans enjoyed considerable standardisation in mortar types with three basic weapons, though production shortfalls ensured that a range of foreign mortars served in both the Wehrmacht and Waffen-SS.

Pieces of foliage have been applied to this whitewashed Hummel during the winter of 1944. By this period of the war much of the burden had fallen on the assault artillery and tank destroyer battalions to try and stem the Red Army onslaught.

Five photographs all showing the s.IG33 artillery gun during action on the Eastern Front in 1944. A typical infantry regiment controlled three infantry battalions, an infantry gun company with six 7.5cm l.IG18 and two 15cm s.IG33 guns, and an anti-tank company with twelve 3.7cm PaK35/36 guns. The 15cm s.IG33 infantry gun was regarded the workhorse pieces operated by specially trained infantrymen.

A mortar crew with the 8cm GW 34 mortar being used against a Soviet target in the snow. This weapon remained the standard German infantry mortar throughout the war. Note that the crew have used their entrenching tool to dig a hole of snow out in order to position the mortar for firing.

SS Panzergrenadiers have earned themselves a bottle of beer each following heavy fighting. During the last two years of the war the number of Panzergrenadier divisions grew and they soon earned the respect of being called the Panzer Elite. With the mounting losses of men and armour, the Panzergrenadiers displayed outstanding ability and endurance in the face of overwhelming odds.

Chapter Four

Bagration and Aftermath

By June 1944, German strategy was faced with a full-fledged two front war. More than fifty-three percent of the army was fighting in Russia, whilst the other forty-seven percent were in Western Europe trying to stem the Allied invasion along the Normandy coast. On the Eastern Front the German Army strength had reached a new low of some 2,242,649 against more than six million Russian troops. The best-equipped and most effective segment of the German force, the *Waffen-SS*, reached a strength of some 400,000 men. Of this total the bulk of the most elite *SS* combat formations were fighting in France. In the East the *SS* were distributed on the northern, central and southern fronts and were intended to act as the backbone of the German fighting machine. Many of its commanders were well aware of the seriousness of the military situation and looked ahead to the coming battles, knowing that that they were bound by orders for which they could not successfully achieve. In front of them stood a huge enemy army whose strength was almost three times their own.

From a trench inside a forest a soldier is armed with a Kar89K bolt action rifle with attached gun sight, and can be seen aiming the weapon at a selected target.

An interesting photograph showing a well camouflaged soldier armed with the lethal *Panzerschreck* or tank shocker. The popular name given by the troops for this weapon was the *Raketenpanzerbüchse* or rocket tank rifle, abbreviated to RPzB. It was an 8.8cm reusable anti-tank rocket launcher developed during the latter half of the war. Another popular nickname was *Ofenrohr* or stove pipe.

During the first week of June reports multiplied as news reached the various German commands that the Russians were preparing a new summer offensive on the central front. By the morning of 22 June 1944, the third anniversary of the invasion of Russia, the long awaited Soviet offensive was launched against *Heeresgruppe Mitte*. In total the First Baltic and Third Belorussian Fronts hurled more than 2.5 million troops, 4,000 tanks, 25,000 artillery pieces and mortars, and 5,300 aircraft to the northwest and southwest of Vitebsk. In opposition the Germans could only field 1,200,000 men, 9,500 guns and 900 tanks, with some 1,300 or so aircraft.

The Russian offensive was code-named 'Operation Bagration', and within twenty-fours hours of the attack Soviet forces had smashed through the lines of *Heeresgruppe Mitte*. In just seven days, the entire length of a 200-mile front stretching from Ostrov on the Lithuanian border and Kovel on the edge of the Pripet Marshes had been completely overrun. In just twelve days *Heeresgruppe Mitte* had lost 25 divisions. Of its original 165,000-man strength, *4.Armee* lost a staggering 130,000 soldiers. The *3.Panzer-Armee* lost 10 divisions. The *9.Armee*, however, held onto its pocket long enough for some 10,000 of its troops to escape

Four photographs in sequence showing a Waffen-SS heavy field howitzer crew preparing their 15cm heavy field howitzer for action. This weapon remained the second most common artillery piece in SS service and served until the end of the war.

the slaughter. In a drastic attempt to stabilise the crumbling lines the 'Totenkopf' division had been rushed north to join the 4.Armee, but became delayed in the chaos and carnage that befell Heeresgruppe Mitte. As the Germans pulled back, the Red Army continued its remorseless drive westwards, carving its way through towards the borders of East Prussia and Poland.

Over the next few weeks Heeresgruppe Mitte drifted westwards towards Kaunas, the Neman River, and Bialystok. The Red Army forces were moving faster than the Germans could deploy its meagre troops, even to attempt a stand. But the Russians having covered more than 200 miles without pause had temporarily outstripped their supplies and as a consequence slowed their advance to a crawl. The Germans, however, took advantage of the situation and tried their best to regroup and plug sectors in the front that had been punched through by the enemy. What was left of Heeresgruppe Mitte was given to feldmarschall Walther Model, known as Hitler's 'fireman'. Model sent the 'Totenkopf' division to the city of Grodno, and there it was ordered to hold the right flank of the 4.Armee in the north, and the left wing of the 2.Armee in the south. Here in the city of Grodno this crack SS division held onto to its crumbling positions, fighting off continuous attacks and bitter street fighting that was reminiscent of some of the close quarter battles that had raged at Stalingrad. However, outnumbered seven to one in troop strength and ten to one in tanks, 'Totenkopf' were gradually ground down in a battle of attrition, and by 18 July requested permission to abandon their receding lines. Model agreed at once and ordered the withdrawal of the division west in the retreat towards the Polish capital, Warsaw.

During the last week of July the Russians pushed forward and rolled across the ravaged countryside of Poland through the shattered German front. On 24 July in the southern sector of the front, the 1.Panzer-Armee still held the town of Lwow and its front to the south. However, behind the Panzer army fifty miles west of Lwow massive Soviet forces were closing to the San River on the stretch between Jaroslaw and Przemysl. Further north in the centre Model had feverishly regrouped his forces in an attempt to defend Siedlce, Warsaw, and the Vistula south to Pulawy. The 'Totenkopf' division was once again thrown into battle this time along with the elite armoured Paratroop Division, known as the 'Herman Goring Felddivisionen'. Both divisions were ordered to hold the city of Siedlce fifty miles east of Warsaw. For four days in the face of strong Russian armoured strikes both divisions with great cost held their lines allowing the 2.Armee to retreat to the Vistula River. On 28 July, they abandoned Siedlce and continued a fighting with-drawal towards Warsaw. Over the coming week fighting in the area was fierce, but both divisions fought to the bitter death slowing the Russian onslaught and allowing Model to reorganise a defence along the river. As for the Soviet forces, having advanced another two hundred miles in two weeks, they had temporarily

Three photographs showing both Waffen-SS and Wehrmacht mortar crews with the 8cm Gr.W.34 mortar. During the war the mortar had become the standard infantry support weapon giving the soldier valuable high explosive capability beyond the range of rifles or grenades. Yet one of the major drawbacks was its accuracy, it being an area weapon. Even with an experienced mortar crew, it generally required 10 bombs to achieve a direct hit on one single target.

German troops in Army group Centre are seen marching. By May 1944 the German forces were holding a battle line more than 1,400 miles in overall length, which had been severely weakened by the overwhelming strength of the Red Army.

outstripped their supplies. The offensive ground to a halt on the Vistula in early August. The brief lull in fighting helped Model to gradually gain strength and re-organise defensive positions. The '*Totenkopf* and the '*Wiking*' divisions formed the *4.Panzer-Korps* commanded by *SS-Gruppenführer* Herbert Gille, and Model placed this *Korps* 30 miles northeast of Warsaw, where he expected the renewal of the Russian offensive.

In side the capital, as news spread that the Russians were drawing closer, the Polish Home Army suddenly revolted and attempted to restore its Polish sover-eignty against the German invaders. The Polish revolt surprised the German command and they quickly brought all available resources they could scrape together to combat the Polish attack. The notorious *Dirlewanger* and *Kaminski* brigades of *SS* irregulars were used against the Warsaw uprising. It was here in the ravaged streets of Warsaw that these *SS* units earned their terrible reputa-tion for a string of atrocities. Here the soldiers were encouraged exploit the situation to the full and turn the streets into a blood bath. Women and children were evacuated from their homes and herded together like animals. In cemeteries, gardens, and squares, the civilians were indiscriminately machine gunned until the frightened mass showed no further sign of life. Within four days of the battle, some 10,000 men, women, and children had been slaughtered in the city, but still the fighting continued.

Whilst the Warsaw uprising was being suppressed the Russians attacked on 14 August northwest of the city and, for several bloody days, the well dug in *Waffen-SS* divisions of 'Totenkopf' and 'Wiking' grimly held out repulsing a number of viscous attacks. The Red Army then regrouped and once again resumed their attack, which fell on 'Totenkopf'. For four days *SS* troops fought a gauntlet of heavy fighting. Russian air support hammered the German frontlines day and night until the 'Totenkopf' and the remainder of the *Panzer-Korps* withdrew from its battered and blasted positions west towards Warsaw. By 10 September heavy fighting engulfed the suburbs of the city with 'Totenkopf' successfully defending its positions. For ten days, until the Red Army offensive petered out, the *SS* managed to hold their lines, in spite of the high losses. During the next few weeks until 10 October there followed a lull in the fighting until the Russians launched yet another offensive, which forced the *4.Panzer-Korps* to retreat twenty-miles west-

A Wehrmacht soldier loads a mortar shell into the Granatwerfer 42 sGW 42 mortar. This was a deadly heavy mortar. The weapon was developed in response to encounters with heavy Soviet mortar of the same calibre and the Germans designed a virtual copy of the Red Army weapon.

A group photograph showing Waffen-SS armed with the Kar98K bolt action rifle and the MG34 machine gun. Although the MG42 surpassed the MG34 by mid-1944, it was still well liked by the crews that used it and remained an integral weapon in both the Wehrmacht and Waffen-SS.

wards. By 27 October the front had once more been stabilised and the Red Army abandoned further assaults against the *4.Panzer-Korps*. Calm returned to the front around Warsaw and both *Wehrmacht* and *Waffen-SS* divisions tended to their wounded, reequipped the best they could and dug another defensive line. '*Totenkopf's*' performance in these defensive battles had demonstrated the effectiveness of using the *Waffen-SS* as a special 'fire brigade' force. They had not only fought off many attacks against an enemy sometime ten-times their strength, but had provided Model's soldiers with a band of men that were able to be rushed from one danger zone to another and plug gaps in the front wherever they appeared. But the German military situation during the summer of 1944 had been a complete disaster in Poland. Although the Soviet advance had been relatively slow, continuously fighting against bitter opposition, the Germans were un-questionably stalling the inevitable defeat in a country that they had conquered and ravaged for almost five years.

Elsewhere on the Eastern Front the situation was equally dire. In the south Malinovsky's 2.Ukrainian Front had broken through powerful German defences, and the Red Army reached the Bulgarian border in early September. Within a week, Russian troops reached the Yugoslav frontier, and on 8 September, Bulgaria and Romania declared war on Germany. By 23 September, Soviet forces arrived on the Hungarian border and immediately raced through the country for the Danube, finally reaching the river to the south of Budapest.

It was here in Hungary that Hitler placed the utmost importance of defending what he called the last bastion of defence in the East. Against all military logic, he felt that it was Hungary and not the Vistula River in Poland, which presented a natural barrier against an advance on Germany. For the defence of Hungary he was determined to use his premier *Waffen-SS* divisions, including '*Totenkopf*' and '*Wiking*' that were positioned along the Vistula River.

Enlisted foreign SS troops march along a dusty road being led by their commander in mid-1944. With severe lack of reinforcements more and more foreign soldiers were enlisted in both Wehrmacht and Waffen-SS divisions to try and bolster the overstretched forces on the Eastern Front.

Chapter Five

Last Battles

In the last months of the war German forces continued receding across a scarred and devastated wasteland. On both the Western and Eastern Fronts, the last agonising moments of the war were played out. Whilst the British and American troops were poised to cross the River Rhine, in the East the terrifying advance of the Red Army was bearing down on the River Oder, pushing back the

A pneumatic boat with a full complement of SS assault troops transporting the boat to a river during operations in 1944. The boat required six troops with paddles and one to steer. They were capable of carrying up to a dozen soldiers including the paddlers.

Three photographs taken in sequence showing Waffen-SS mortar troops during operations in mid-1944. By this period of the war the German soldier had expended considerable combat efforts and lacked sufficient reconnaissance and the necessary support of tanks and heavy weapons to compensate for the large losses sustained.

SS troops have expertly positioned their 8.8cm FlaK gun in a defensive position. By 1944 a typical SS Panzer-Division was authorized 80 towed and 40 self-propelled 2cm guns, six cm quad weapons, nine 3.7cm guns and 12 heavy 8.8cm flak pieces. Less, well-equipped grenadier and Gebirgsjäger-Divisions had 18 towed and 12 self-propelled 2cm guns.

last remnants of Hitler's exhausted units. The resistance of her once mighty armies were now collapsing amid the ruins of the *Reich*. Most of the so called *Waffen-SS* crack divisions were still embroiled in heavy fighting in Hungary and were unable to be released in order to plug the massive gaps on the German front lines in the East. This left the northern and central sectors of the Eastern Front to east and west SS European volunteers. Many of the volunteers, spurred on by the worrying prospect of Russian occupation of Europe and certain death if captured, were determined to defend to the bitter end and try to hold back the Red Army advance.

The last great offensive that brought the Russians their final victory in the East began during the third week of January 1945. The principal objective was to crush the remaining German forces in Poland, East Prussia and the Baltic states. Along the Baltic an all-out Russian assault had begun in earnest with the sole intention to crush the remaining understrength German units that had once formed *Heeresgruppe Nord*. It was these heavy, sustained attacks that eventually restricted the German-held territory in the north-east to a few small pockets of land surrounding three ports: Libau, Kurland, Pillau in East Prussia and Danzig at the mouth of the River Vistula.

Here along the Baltic the German defenders attempted to stall the massive Russian push with the remaining weapons and men they had at their disposal. Every German soldier defending the area was aware of the significance if it was captured. Not only would the coastal garrisons be cut off and eventually destroyed, but also masses of civilian refugees would be prevented from escaping from those ports by sea. Hitler made it quite clear that all remaining *Wehrmacht*, *Waffen-SS* volunteer units, and *Luftwaffe* personnel were not to evacuate, but to stand and fight and wage an unprecedented battle of attrition. In fact, what Hitler had done by a single sentence was to condemn to death 8,000 officers and more than 181,000 soldiers and *Luftwaffe* personnel.

In southwest Poland situated on the River Oder the strategic town of Breslau had been turned into a fortress and defended by various *Volkssturm*, *Hitlerjugend*, *Waffen-SS* and various formations from the 269.Infantry-Division. During mid-February 1945 the German units put up a staunch defence with every available weapon that they could muster. As the battle ensued, both German soldiers and civilians were cut to pieces by Russian attacks. During these viscous battles, which endured until May 1945, there were many acts of courageous fighting. Cheering and yelling, old men and boys of the *Volkssturm* and *Hitlerjugend*, supported by ad hoc *SS* units, advanced across open terrain, sacrificing themselves in front of well-positioned Russian machine gunners and snipers. By the first week of March,

An MG34 machine gunner and his feeder inside a house during intensive fighting. During the opening phase of the Soviet summer offensive, code-named 'Operation Bagration', the German soldier was ill prepared against any type of large-scale offensive.

German troops withdraw across a river in Army Group Centre during 'Bagration'. Commanders in the field were fully aware of the significant problems and the difficulties imposed by committing badly-equipped soldiers to defend the depleted lines of defence.

Russian infantry had driven back the defenders into the inner city and were pulverising it street by street. Lightly clad *SS*, *Volkssturm* and *Hitlerjugend* were still seen resisting, forced to fight in the sewers beneath the decimated city. When defence of Breslau finally capitulated almost 60,000 Russian soldiers were killed or wounded trying to capture the town, with some 29,000 German military and civilian casualties.

Elsewhere on the Eastern Front, fighting was merciless, with both sides imposing harsh measures on their men to stand where they were and fight to the death. In the *Wehrmacht* and *Waffen-SS* volunteer divisions, all malingerers were hanged by the roadside without even a summary court martial. Those who deserted or caused self-inflicted wounds were executed on the spot. Soldiers would regularly pass groups of freshly erected gallows, where the *SS* and *Feldgendarmerie* had hanged deserters. Signs were tied around their necks, some of them reading:

'Here I hang because I did not believe in the *Führer*'

With every defeat and withdrawal came ever-increasing pressure on the commanders to exert harsher discipline on their weary men. The thought of fighting on German soil for the first time resulted in mixed feelings among the soldiers. Although the defence of the *Reich* automatically stirred emotional feelings to fight for their land, not all soldiers felt the same way. More and more young conscripts were showing signs that they did not want to die for a lost cause. Conditions on the Eastern Front were miserable not only for the newest recruits, but also for battle-hardened soldiers who had survived many months of bitter conflict against the Red Army. The cold harsh weather during February and March prevented the soldiers digging trenches more than a metre down. But the main problems that confronted the German forces during this period were shortages of ammunition, fuel and vehicles. Some vehicles in a division could only be used in an emergency and battery fire was strictly prohibited without permission from the commanding officer. The daily ration on average per division was for two shells per gun.

With such drastic restrictions of every kind, tens of thousands of undernourished civilians, mostly women, alongside remaining slave labourers, were marched out to expend all their available energy to dig lines of anti-tank ditches. Most of the ditches were dug between the Vistula and Oder Rivers, as a secondary line of defence. However, German forces were now barely holding the wavering Vistula positions that ran some 175 miles from the Baltic coast to the juncture of the Oder and Neisse in Silesia. Most of the front was now held on the western bank of the Oder. In the north, the ancient city of Stettin, capital of Pomerania, and in the south, the town of Kustrin, were both vital holding points against the main Russian objective of the war – Berlin.

A 7.5cm l.IG18 is seen here in action. This particular weapon was used in direct infantry support. The gun was very versatile in combat and the crew often aggressively positioned it, which usually meant the piece was regularly exposed on the battlefield.

A heavy MG34 machine gun position with the MG on a sustained fire mount during intensive fighting against strong Russian forces. This position is along one of the many defensive belts constructed along the front in Army Group Centre.

As the great Red Army drive gathered momentum, more towns and villages fell to the onrushing forces. Suicidal opposition from a few *SS* and *Wehrmacht* strong points bypassed in earlier attacks reduced buildings to blasted rubble. Everywhere it seemed the Germans were being constantly forced to retreat. Many isolated units spent hours or even days fighting a bloody defence. Russian soldiers frequently requested them to surrender and assured them that no harm would come to them if they did so. But despite this reassuring tone, most German troops continued to fight to the bitter end. To the German soldier in 1945 they were fighting an enemy that they not only despised, but also were terrified of. Many soldiers, especially those fighting in the ranks of the *Waffen-SS* decided that their fate would be met out on the battlefield. To them they would rather bleed fighting on the grasslands of Eastern Europe than surrender and be at the mercy of a Russian soldier.

By the end of March the bulk of the German forces that once consisted of *Heeresgruppe Mitte*, and was now known as *Heeresgruppe* Vistula were manned by many inexperienced training units. Some soldiers were so young that in their rations they had sweets instead of tobacco. All of them were ordered to stand and fight and not to abandon their positions. Terrified at the prospect of retreating, which would warrant almost certain execution if they did so, many reluctantly opted to bury themselves deep into a foxhole or bunker. Here they hoped the Soviet attackers would give them a chance to surrender, instead of burning them alive with flamethrowers or blowing them to pieces by hand grenade.

By early April the atmosphere among the troops of *Heeresgruppe* Vistula became a mixture of terrible foreboding and despair as the Russians prepared to push forward on the River Oder. Here along the Oder and Neisse fronts the troops waited for the front to become engulfed by the greatest concentration of firepower ever amassed by the Russians. General Zhukov's 1st Belorussian Front and General Konev's 1st Ukrainian Front were preparing to attack German forces defending positions east of Berlin. For the attack the Red Army mustered some 2.5 million men, divided into four armies. They were supported by 41,600 guns and heavy mortars as well as 6,250 tanks and self-propelled guns.

The final battle before Berlin began at dawn on 16 April 1945. Just thirty-eight miles east of the German capital above the swollen River Oder, red flares burst into the night sky, triggering a massive artillery barrage. For nearly an hour, an eruption of flame and smoke burst along the German front. Then, in the mud, smoke, and darkness, the avalanche broke. In an instant, General Zhukov's soldiers were compelled to stumble forward into action. As they surged forward, the artillery barrage remained in front of them, covering the area ahead.

A group of troops use a bomb crater as cover during heavy unrelenting fighting. After more than four days of constant fighting Hitler refused to permit his force to tactically withdraw and contained them in fixed defensive positions that inevitably led to Red Army rifle divisions encircling and destroying them with relative ease.

A mortar crew withdrawing from yet another position as the Red Army wrench-open the front lines of Army Group Centre in late June 1944.

Under the cover of darkness on the night of 15th April, most German forward units had been moved back to a second line just before the expected Russian artillery barrage. In this second line, as the first rays of light prevailed across the front, soldiers waited for the advancing Russians. Along the entire front dispersed among the 3. and 9.Armee's they had fewer than 700 tanks and self-propelled guns. The heaviest division, the 25.Panzer, had just 79 such vehicles: the smallest unit had just two. Artillery too was equally poor with only 744 guns. Ammunition and fuel were in a critical state of supply and reserves in some units were almost non-existent. Opposing the main Russian assault stood the 56.Panzer-Korps. It was under the command of General Karl Weidling, known to his friends as 'smasher Karl'. Weidling had been given the awesome task of preventing the main Russian breakthrough in the area.

When the Soviet forces finally attacked during the early morning of 16 April, the Germans were ready to meet them on the Seelow Heights. From the top of the ridge, hundreds of German flak guns that had been hastily transferred from the Western Front poured a hurricane of fire into the enemy troops. All morning, shells and gunfire rained down on the Red Army, blunting their assault. By dusk the Russians, savagely mauled by the attack, fell back. It seemed the Red Army had under-estimated the strength and determination of their enemy.

By the next day, the Russians had still not breached the German defences. But General Zhukov, with total disregard of casualties, was determined to batter the enemy into submission and ruthlessly bulldoze his way through. Slowly and systematically the Red Army began smashing through their opponents. Within hours hard-pressed and exhausted German troops were feeling the full brunt of the assault. Confusion soon swept the decimated lines. Soldiers who had fought doggedly from one fixed position to another were now seized with panic.

In three days of constant fighting, thousands of German soldiers had perished. Despite their attempts to blunt the Red Army, the road to Berlin was finally wrenched wide open. At this crucial moment a number of top quality *SS* soldiers had been gathered in the recently established *11.Panzer-Armee* under the command of *SS-Obergruppenführer* Felix Steiner. The *11.Panzer-Armee* had been given the task of launching an offensive designed to dislocate the threatened enemy advance on Berlin, but had been halted against massive attacks. When the final push on Berlin begun on 16 April, the *11.Panzer-Armee* retained only three reliable divisions. One of these, the 18.Panzergrenadier-Division, was transferred from east of Berlin. A few days later the 11.*SS*.Panzergrenadier-Division 'Nordland' was rushed to Berlin and the *SS* Brigade '*Nederland*' was sent out of the capital to help stem the Russian advance. Inside the ruined city, part of the 15.Waffengrenadier-Division der *SS* from Latvia was ordered to take up

A heavy MG34 machine gun on a sustained fire mount along a defensive position. Even during Bagration German infantry could have considerable staying power against enemy infantry as long as they kept their weapon operational and deployed in good fields of fire.

defensive positions together with the Belgian 'Langemarck' and 'Wallonien' Divisions, and the remaining volunteers of the French 'Charlemagne' Division. All of these Waffen-SS troops were to take part in the last, apocalyptic struggle to save the Reich capital from the clutches of the Red Army.

By 25 April Berlin was completely surrounded, and the next day some half a million Soviet troops bulldozed their way through the city. Beneath the Reich Chancellery building, which had now become Hitler's home and headquarters, the Führer was determined to save the crumbling capital and had already ordered remnants of SS-Obergruppenführer Felix Steiner's 11.Panzer-Armee to attack immediately from their positions in the Eberswalde, then to drive south, cutting off the Russian assault on Berlin. On Hitler's map, the plan looked brilliant. But it was impossible to gather forces to make Steiner's SS Kampfgruppe even remotely operational. Steiner himself wrote that the forces at his disposal amounted to less than a weak Korps. He was well aware that his attack would receive little or no support as the 9.Armee was completely surrounded and the 12.Armee consisted

A Flak gunner stands next to his 2cm FlaK gun outside the town of Orsha during a lull in the heavy fighting in Army Group Centre. The defence of Orsha was bitterly contested by the 78th Assault Division, but neither the manpower nor weaponry could hold back the overwhelming enemy.

only of a few battered divisions. As for Hitler's reinforcements they consisted of fewer than 5,000 *Luftwaffe* personnel and *Hitlerjugend*, all armed with hand-held weapons. The city was doomed.

For the next week the battle for Berlin raged. True to their motto, 'My Honour is my Loyalty', the *Waffen-SS* were seen fighting bitterly with members of the *Hitlerjugend, Volkssturm, Luftwaffe* and *Wehrmacht* troops. Here the soldiers were ordered to fight to the death and anyone found deserting or shirking from their duties were hunted down by *Reichsführer* Heinrich Himmler's personal Escort battalion and hanged from the nearest lamppost. But even in the last days of the war both the Wehrmacht and the *SS* proved to be an efficient, formidable and ruthless fighting machine. Even as the last hours were fought out in the fiery cauldron of Berlin, German units, lacking all provisions including many types of weapons, effectively halted and stemmed a number of Russian assaults.

Waffen-SS troops rest in a field. With their distinctive camouflage smocks the troops blend well in the local terrain.

Troops of the SS. Wiking-Division in a crop field in the summer of 1944. The division had suffered heavy losses in the East and would soon be withdrawn into Poland in the defensive battles around Warsaw.

Troops of the SS. Wiking-Division pose for the camera in a defensive position. By 1944 the qualities of the Wiking division as a combat unit were already testified by the number of Knight's Crosses of the Iron Cross awarded to its soldiers.

An interesting photograph showing SS troops passing a halted Panther V in 1944. The soldiers are armed with a variety of weapons including the MG42 machine gun, Panzerfaust, and the Stumgewehr 44 assault rifle.

Well camouflaged soldiers of the SS.Wiking Division in July 1944. By this stage of the war the Wikingers had attained an elite status equal to the best of the original Waffen-SS divisions.

A StuG.III belonging to the Waffen-SS has halted on a road. By 1944 the StuG.III had become an extremely common assault gun, especially on the Eastern Front. By this period of the war the StuG had been slowly absorbed into Panzer units, Panzer and Panzergrenadier divisions of the Wehrmacht and Waffen-SS.

Two Waffen-SS soldiers armed with the Kar98K bolt action rifle are in a defensive position somewhere in Poland in 1944. A line of stick grenades are also close at hand. In spite of the disintegrating front, the SS fought well in Poland and managed to win a number of defensive battles.

Waffen-SS troops armed with an MG42 and Kar98K rifle have captured two Soviet soldiers hiding in hay during heavy engagements along the frontier of East Prussia where staunch German defences helped halt the Russian onslaught.

SS troops during the defence of Poland inthe late winter of 1944. Although the military situation for both the SS and Wehrmacht looked dire, staunch resistance in many places in the East was actually slowing down the Russian advance.

An MG42 machine gunner and feeder overlooking the Baltic Sea during the battle of the Baltic's in late 1944. During the last weeks of 1944, the German Army was still fighting on foreign soil. Exhausted and demoralised skeletal units that had been waging a battle of attrition for months were now fully aware of the impending defeat.

Wehrmacht troops wearing green splinter army reversible camouflage uniforms inside an inflatable boat move across a river in order to set up a new defensive position. One soldier can be seen armed with the Sturmgewehr 44. This fine weapon was concentrated mainly in special Wehrmacht and Waffen-SS counterattack units.

In the snow a soldier can be seen with a tripod-mounted range finder. This device was able to calculate the approximate height and distance of an object either on the ground or air by a series of grid references imposed on the field of view. Once determined, the information could then be quickly given to the flak crew who would aim accordingly. Behind the soldier is an 8.8cm FlaK gun being used against a ground target.

A heavy MG34 machine gun position on a sustained fire mount in Poland in late 1944. In Poland Army Group Centre was dangerously understrength and faced an overwhelming enemy army. The Red Army had a numerical superiority of 11 to 1 in infantry, 7 to 1 in armour and a massive 20 to 1 in artillery.

Wehrmacht troops pose for the camera in a defensive position in Poland in late 1944. During this period the 3rd Panzer Army and 4th Army were holding in the north while to the southwest, along the Narev River, the 2nd Army was fiercely contesting every foot of ground.

An Sd.kfz.251 makes its way through a village during intensive heavy fighting. The Sd.Kfz.251 had become not just a halftrack intended to simply transport infantry to the edge of the battlefield, but also a fully-fledged fighting vehicle.

A white-washed 7.5cm PaK40 is positioned in a log-frame shelter with the crew. Such shelters offered no real protection from enemy fire, but did protect the gun, ammunition, and crew from the rain and snow. It also provided a degree of concealment as well.

Soldiers dressed in Greatcoats near to the front lines. They are armed with the Kar98K bolt action rifle and two of the men are carrying ammunition boxes for their Mausers.

An SS mortar crew march in the snow. The soldiers have no winter protection, which probably suggests they are on a training exercise with their commander before going back to the front lines.

A white-washed FlaK gun and crew wearing full winter camouflage smocks in a defensive position against ground targets. The end of 1944 ended with the German Army still fighting on foreign soil trying desperately to gain the initiative and throw back the Red Army from its remorseless drive on the German frontier.

Three photographs showing mortar crews in action along the Vistula in early 1945. As the whole military campaign in the East collapsed it was proposed that all German forces located between the Oder and Vistula rivers be amalgamated into a new army group. It was to be named Arm Group Vistula and its commander would be no other than *SS-Reichsführer* Heinrich Himmler.

Two photographs taken in sequence showing troops wearing winter camouflage smocks lying in the snow during fighting in Army Group Vistula in late January 1945. It was here across vast expanses of frozen terrain that the Wehrmacht soldiers together with the Waffen-SS were supposed to prevent the Soviets from breaking through and reaching the frontiers of the Reich.

A Waffen-SS heavy MG34 position on a sustained fire mount. The Red army's winter offensive in January 1945 was so fierce that on the first day of the attack it had actually ripped open a breach more than twenty-miles wide in the Vistula Front. Both Waffen-SS and Wehrmacht troops tried desperately to contain the advancing Russian forces.

StuG.III's advance along a snow covered road with grenadiers hitching a lift onboard. Despite the longer 7.5cm barrel this assault gun was continually hard pressed on the battlefield and constantly called upon for offensive and defensive fire support, where it was gradually compelled to operate increasingly in an anti-tank roll.

A PaK crew with their white-washed PaK35/36 anti-tank gun in a defensive role. German strategy faced its ultimate challenge in the East as the Red Army smashed its way towards the borders of the Reich.

Wehrmacht troops on sleds in Army Group North in January 1945. By this period of the war there was a mood of near desperation, but luckily for the Germans the ice and snow hindered the Russian onslaught.

Two photographs taken in sequence showing German troops passing through a village and following the scorched Earth order from their commanders by setting alight to all the buildings. The scorched earth policy was a military strategy or operational method which involved destroying anything that might be useful to the enemy while advancing through or withdrawing from an area.

An Sdk.Kfz.251 halftrack advances along a road. Throughout the war the performance of the grenadiers and Panzergrenadiers in battle was attributed mainly to the halftrack, which transported infantry units onto the battlefield. Even during the last desperate months of the war, the halftrack was used extensively to ferry men and material back and forth to the front line.

One of the quickest and effective methods of moving across the snow was by sled. Here a FlaK gun has been mounted on a sled and has been pressed into action against an enemy target in early 1945.

During the defence of the homeland in 1945. Two Wehrmacht officers confer whilst behind them grenadiers can be seen moving towards the front. An Sd.Kfz.251/9 is armed with the powerful 7.5cm KwK 37 L/24.

On the Oder Front a group of troops converse in the early spring of 1945. It was on 30 March on the Oder Front, that German troops finally evacuated their last remaining bridgehead at Wollin just north of Stettin, leaving the town to be captured by Russian forces.

Waffen-SS troops pose for the camera before resuming operations on the front lines against overwhelming superiority of the Red Army.

An unidentified SS unit, probably in the Nord-Division during operations in the Baltic's during the last months of the war. The soldiers fought courageously and battled from one receding front to another.

Two photographs taken in sequence showing infantry ferrying supplies across a river. Onboard are loaves of bread, which was a vital ingredient to the dwindling stocks of food supplied to the German forces in the Ost. An MG34 mounted on an anti-aircraft tripod is being used against possible aerial attack.

A column of vehicles carrying supplies and troops has halted on a road near the Oder. Troops can be seen standing next to a stream.

SS troops withdrawn across an open carrying with them ammunition boxes. By March 1945 the bulk of the Eastern Front was being supported by many inexperienced soldiers. All of them though were ordered to stand and fight and not abandon their positions.

Inside a forest clearing and SS soldiers pose for a group photograph with their mosquito nets temporarily pulled back over their headdress. With the vast amounts of lakes and stagnated pools of water in the forested regions of the Baltics and northern Russia, mosquitoes plagued the daily routine of the German soldier.

The crew of a 10.5cm artillery gun have positioned their weapon inside a town in eastern Germany. By early April the German Army dug-in as the Russians prepared to smash across the Oder and reach Berlin. The atmosphere among the troops had become a mixture of terrible foreboding and despair.

An 8cm sGrW 34 mortar crew in action against an enemy target during the battle of the Reich in March/April 1945. By this period of the war suicidal opposition from the last remaining SS and Wehrmacht strong points were being grimly held at all costs. Many isolated units spent hours or even days fighting a bloody defence and were slowly ground down by the sheer superiority of the Soviet colossus.

Appendices

Appendix One

Waffen-SS

Weapons and Equipment

The bulk of the weapons and equipment used by the *Waffen-SS* throughout the war was more or less identical to that used by the *Wehrmacht*. A number of small arms, particularly those of foreign origin, saw considerable use in the units of the *Waffen-SS* due to the *Wehrmacht's* reluctance to supply sufficient quantities of German-produced hard wear to Himmler's elite force. The *Waffen-SS* used a huge variety of weaponry, everything from small arms to heavy tanks. The elite *SS* Panzer divisions, especially, were equipped with Germany's best tanks and supporting armoured vehicles. From 1943 onward, *Waffen-SS* troops were normally the first to be furnished with a host of new modern weaponry. However, even these elite troops were curtailed by never-ending shortages and were supplied with various weapons and equipment in order to sustain them on the battlefield long enough to drive back the growing enemy forces.

During the last two years of the war the *Waffen-SS* supplemented the finest hardware the German armaments industry could produce with many standard popular weapons and equipment used by their *Wehrmacht* counterparts. Below are the principle types of weaponry used by the Waffen-SS, especially during the last two years of the war. The Wehrmacht also used a wide variety of these weapons and equipment too.

Popular Waffen-SS Weapons and Equipment
SMALL ARMS

Pistole 08 Pistol or Luger
Pisztoly 37M Hungarian Service Pistol
Frommer 7.65mm Hungarian Pistol
Model 1914 Norwegian Service Pistol
Fallschirmjäger 42 Automatic Rifle
Maschinenkarabiner 42
Gewehr 41 (W) Self-Loading Rifle

Maschinenpistole (MP) 28
Maschinenpistole (MP) 43
Sturmgewehr 44 (Assault Rifle)
Maschinenpistole (MP) 38
Maschinenpistole (MP) 40
Kar 98K Bolt-Action Rifle

INFANTRY SUPPORT WEAPONS

Maschinengewehr 34 (MG)
Maschinengewehr 42 (MG)
5cm Leichte Granatwerfer (leGW) 36 Mortar
15cm Nebelwerfer 41 (NbW 41)
21cm Nebelwerfer 42 (NbW 42)
Flammenwerfer (FlW) 41
Steilhandgrenate 39
Anti-tank and Anti-aircraft Weapons
7.92mm Panzerb?sche 38 Anti-Tank Rifle
7.92mm Panzerb?sche 39 Anti-Tank Rifle
3.7cm Pak 35/36 Anti-Tank Gun
5cm Pak 38 Anti-Tank Gun
7.5cm Pak 40 Heavy Anti-Tank Gun
8.8cm Pak 43 Heavy Anti-Tank Gun
Faustpatrone 30 Anti-Tank Rocket
Raketenpanzerb?sche (RPzB) 54 Anti-Tank Rocket Launcher
2cm Flugabwehrkanone (Flak) 30
2cm Flugabwehrkanone (Flak) 38
8.8cm Flugabwehrkanone (Flak) 18

ARTILLERY

10.5cm leFH 18 Light Field Howitzer
7.5cm Leichte Feldkanone 18 (leFK)
7.5cm Feldkanone 40 (FK 40)
10cm Kanone 18 (s 10cm K 18)
15cm Schwere Feldhaubitze 18 (sFH 18)
21cm M?rser 18 (21cm Mrs 18) Heavy Gun

Armoured Cars and Halftracks

ARMOURED CARS

Sd.Kfz.221
Sd.Kfz.222
Sd.Kfz.223
Sd.Kfz.231
Sd.Kfz.234
Sd.Kfz.260
Sd.Kfz.261
Sd.Kfz.263

ARTILLERY PRIME MOVER HALFTRACKS

Sd.Kfz.2
Sd.Kfz.6
Sd.Kfz.7
Sd.Kfz.8
Sd.Kfz.9
Sd.Kfz.10
Sd.Kfz.11

LIGHT ARMOURED RECONNAISSANCE HALFTRACKS

Sd.Kfz.250 Series (12 Variants)

LIGHT AMMUNITION CARRIER HALFTRACK

Sd.Kfz.252
Sd.Kfz.253

MEDIUM ARMOURED PERSONNEL CARRIER HALFTRACK

Sd.Kfz.251 (22 Variants)

PANZERS

Pz.Kpfw.III (Later Variants)
Pz.Kpfw.IV (Later Variants)
Pz.Kpfw.V Panther
Pz.Kpfw.VI. Tiger.I
Pz.Kpfw.VI. Tiger.II

Sturmgeschütz (StuG.III) (Later Variants)
Sturmgeschütz (StuG.IV)
Panzerjager Marder.I
Panzerjäger Marder.II
Panzerjäger Marder.III
Panzerjäger Nashorn
Panzerjäger Hummel
Panzerjäger Wespe
Jagdpanzer.IV/70 Tank Destroyer
Jagdpanzer.38 (t) Hetzer
Jagdpanzer. V Jagdpanther

Infantry Division 1944

By 1944 the infantry division had gone through a series of changes and had been modified and reorganised. The reconnaissance battalion for instance was removed and introduced with a bicycle mounted reconnaissance platoon within every regiment. The anti-tank battalion was more or less made motorised and consisted of an anti-tank company equipped with Jagdpanzer IVs, Hetzers or StuG's, which were organised into three platoons of 4 vehicles and an HQ section of 2 vehicles, a motorised anti-tank company of 12 x 7.5cm Pak 40 guns and a motorised flak company equipped with 12 x 2cm or 3.7cm flak guns. The engineer battalion also took over the responsibility of the heavy weapons company. It comprised of three engineer companies, each equipped with 2 x 81cm mortars, 2 x MG's and 6 portable flamethrowers. The heavy weapons in the engineer battalion was normally mounted in trucks, but by 1944 they were predominately pulled by animal draught, whilst the troops would be mounted on bicycles.

At regimental level an anti-tank company was added. This consisted of a platoon equipped with 3 x 5cm Pak 38 guns and 2 platoons armed with Panzerfausts. Within the regiments, the infantry battalion was reduced in size to just two. A number of divisions in the field were attached with fusilier battalions and were structured identically to the new standard rifle battalion. The infantry battalions were equipped with 4 x 12cm heavy mortars, whilst the rifle companies heavy weapons platoon were equipped with 2 x 8.1cm mortars.

The Panzergrenadier Division 1944

By 1944 many infantry divisions were re-designated as Panzergrenadier divisions. Although having an armoured designation, the Panzergrenadier division was still technically an infantry formation. However, unlike a normal infantry division there was a higher than usual attachment of armoured vehicles. A typical Panzergrenadier division had at least one battalion of infantry that were transported to the forward edge of the battlefield by Sd.kfz.251 halftracks, and various armoured support provided by its own StuG battalion. A typical Panzergrenadier division normally composed an HQ company, a motorised engineer battalion and two Panzergrenadier regiments. Invariably a Panzergrenadier division had a StuG

Battalion, which contained an HQ platoon equipped with 3 StuG's and 3 StuG Companies. The StuG battalion was normally supported by a company comprising of a StuG platoon which was equipped with 4 x StuG's with 10.5cm guns, a flak platoon with 3 x quad 2cm guns mounted on Sd.Kfz.6 or 7 halftracks, an armoured engineer platoon with 5 x Sd.Kfz.250 halftracks, and a motorised signal platoon. Other support elements with the divisions comprised of the following:

ARTILLERY REGIMENT

3 x 2cm Flak Guns towed by a howitzer battalion
3 x 2cm Flak Guns
4 x 15cm sFH 18 Howitzers
4 x 10.5cm leFH 18 Howitzers
1 battery of 6 x Hummel's
2 batteries of 6 x Wespe's
1 Company of 14 x Jagdpanzers
15 x 7.5cm Pak 40 vehicle towed Guns
1 Company of 12 x Quad Flak 2cm Guns
2 Companies of 4 x 8.8cm Guns

ARMOURED RECONNAISSANCE BATTALION

4 Platoons of 4 x Sd.Kfz.231
MG Platoons of 4 x MG 34/42 [on sustained fire mounts]
3 x Rifle Platoons

ARMOURED RECONNAISSANCE BATTALION SUPPORT

2 x 7.5cm le IG 18 Guns
3 x 5cm Pak 38 Guns
1 x Engineer Platoon

Panzer/Panzergrenadier-Brigade July 1944

By early July 1944 as the situation in Army Group Centre deteriorated Hitler outlined that his forces needed small, mobile, fast armoured Kampfgruppe, which could be used effectively in action to meet the attacking enemy armoured formations. During the first week of July plans were issued to create these special armoured Kampfgruppe. They were to consist of at least one SPW-Battalion; one Panzer group with some 40 Panzers, one Pak Company and a number of flak wagons. In total about twelve such Kampfgruppe, named as Panzer-Brigades, were to be issued to fighting units on the Eastern Front.

On 11 July OKH issued orders to create ten Panzer Brigades and these were designated as Panzer-Brigade 101 to 110. Each Panzer-Brigade had one Panzer

Abteilung with three Panther companies and one Panzer Jaeger Company, one Panzergrenadier Battalion with four companies.

Wehrmacht Panzer-Division (1944)

PANZER DIVISION HQ

Reconnaissance Battalion
Self-Propelled Anti-Tank Battalion
Combat Engineers Battalion
Anti-Aircraft Artillery Battalion
Tank Regiment
Tank Battalion
Tank Battalion
Mechanized Infantry Regiment
Mechanized Infantry Battalion
Road Motorized Infantry Battalion
Mechanized Infantry Regiment
Road Motorized Infantry Battalion
Infantry Battalion
Artillery Regiment
Artillery Battalion
Artillery Battalion
Artillery Battalion

Appendix Three

Combat Uniforms of the Waffen-SS 1943–45

General Information Notes

This section is not to give a definite reference to the combat uniforms worn by all the Waffen-SS divisions that saw active service during the latter half of the war, but simply to supply the reader with the general uniforms seen on the battle front between 1943–45.

TUNICS

The Waffen-SS service uniforms worn between 1943–45 were generally designed in the typical army pattern M1940 tunic. They were field-grey in colour and manufactured from wool/rayon mixed material. They had four box pleated patch pockets. The collar patches displayed the typical wartime machine embroidered runes or insignia of the attached division. The shoulder straps were piped in a number of various colours depending on rank. On the left sleeve was the standard machine-embroidered eagle and chevron displaying the rank. The most prominent piece of insignia was the cuff title worn by all premier SS formations. The lesser divisions, or better known as non-German volunteer SS divisions wore tunics that varied considerably in quality. The design of the tunic was almost universal, but the volunteers, presumably to retain the individual soldiers national pride, normally wore the divisional emblem patch on the right collar, the national arm shield and the cuff title.

CAMOUFLAGE SMOCKS AND UNIFORMS

The Waffen-SS were the first soldiers in the World to be issued with camouflage clothing on a large scale. These camouflage printed uniforms became as much the hallmark of the Waffen-SS as the runes worn on their collars. The patterns, however, were quite varied and as a consequence multitude camouflage patterns were developed through the war. The camouflage jacket or smock was a very popular piece of uniform and was supposed to be worn over the wool service uniform and the field equipment. This loose fitting reversible smock was made from a high quality water-repellent cotton duck material, one side usually screened printed in spring/summer colour scheme and the reverse showing autumn/winter colours. From 1943 onwards the camouflage patterns varied considerably from the early type 1940 oakleaf camouflage smock, the M1942 second type oakleaf and palm tree camouflage smocks, M1943 'pea' pattern drill camouflage uniform, to the M1944 'pea' pattern camouflage drill uniform. It was not uncommon to see *Waffen-SS* soldiers in 1943–45, wearing a combination of the M1943 drill and M1944 herringbone twill camouflage uniforms. The difference in colours was quite apparent between the predominately ochre yellow 1943 jacket or trousers and the pinkish brown hue of the 1944 trousers or jacket.

Another item of camouflage clothing worn by the Waffen-SS during the war was the M1937 style camouflage tunic. It was made of herringbone twill, printed with 'pea' pattern camouflage and resembled the classic M37 tunic, since it had pleated breast pockets with flaps lined with artificial silk.

In 1944, the camouflage blouse was introduced. This waist length blouse roughly resembled the M1944 *feldbluse* or the British battledress blouse in cut, though with open patch pockets. It was made from *Zeltbahn* material, with autumn colours on the outside, but was not reversible.

WINTER UNIFORMS

The most universal item of winter clothing worn by the *Waffen-SS* was the two-piece snowsuit. This shapeless two-piece snowsuit consisting of a white jacket and white trousers were commonly worn by the SS, especially the volunteer combat formations. Another form of white snow camouflage clothing was the long overall coat, which buttoned right down the front of the garment. Large and shapeless it was worn without a belt over any uniform and all the equipment. However, the snowsuit tended to restrict the wearers freedom of movement and was not very popular by late 1943.

One of the most popular items of clothing in the winter was the reversible padded winter uniform, which was worn by both the *Wehrmacht* and *Waffen-SS* in the later war years. This padded grey/white suit was produced in the winter of 1942 43, and was the first truly reversible cold weather uniform offering both concealment and extra warmth to become available to the troops on the Eastern Front in large numbers. Originally the suit was in grey-green, although the SS had them produced in a darker steel grey colour.

Another garment worn by the SS in the later war period was the Italian fur-lined, padded over-jacket, which was made from captured Italian camouflage material in 1944. The jacket was made large enough to be worn over the field equipment, so that a soldiers weapons and ammunition could also be kept warm in the extreme arctic conditions. In the cold weather the hood could be easily tightened around the head and helmet.

Panzer Uniform

The most common armoured uniform worn by the Panzer units of the Waffen-SS was the special black armoured crew uniform. The SS Panzer uniforms varied from that of the army version, and consisted of small and more rounded lapels and lacked the pink upper lapel piping initially worn by all army ranks. The black uniform was a very practical garment for all types of duty and was still seen in 1943 when the camouflage clothing specifically for armoured crews were introduced.

The armoured crews camouflage overalls were designed entirely for concealment when the crewman was away from his vehicle. The overall was reversible with autumn browns inside, and a green oakleaf type pattern for the spring and summer.

Another popular variation of the armoured uniform was the reed-green two-piece garment. However, by January 1944, it was decided to replace it with a two-piece printed 'pea' pattern camouflage version. There were three slightly different models manufactured, but the cut did not vary.

Assault Gun Uniform

When designing the uniform for crews of tank destroyers and self-propelled assault guns serving in the Panzer and Panzergrenadier divisions, the Germans decided on using the same style and practical cut of the black Panzer uniform to produce a new version, known as the self-propelled gun crew uniform. This special uniform was made entirely of field-grey cloth with all the details of cut and design as those of the black Panzer uniform. However, the uniform did differ in respect to the SS collar insignia.

Another variation of the assault gun uniform, but introduced in the later part of the war was the 'pea' style herringbone camouflage jacket with pointed lapels.

Steel Helmet

The most distinctive universal headgear issued to the *Waffen-SS* was the steel helmet. In particular during the second half of the war the SS wore three major models, the basic M1935 and M1940 to the final M1942 pattern. By 1943 most of the steel helmets were predominantly covered with camouflage cloth that were held on by an envelope of material that slipped over the peak, and by three small sprung clips, one either side and one at the rear. The fabric, normally matching the camouflage smock, was printed on both sides in contrasting seasonal colour schemes for spring/summer and autumn/winter. However, even by 1943 there were still *Waffen-SS* soldiers, including those in the premier *SS* divisions that wore the single decal steel helmets without the camouflage fabric covering. The helmets had their previous shiny surface removed by soldiers daubing them with mud and camouflaging them with anything available, from vehicle paint to winter whitewash. In fact, by 1943 some artistic *SS* troops begun to mimic the various dot camouflage uniform patterns by applying paint to the helmet while covering it with chicken wire netting. The colours varied, but on many examples soldiers applied browns, greens and ochre's that were colours specifically issued to camouflage vehicles from mid-1943 onwards.

Combat Uniforms of the Wehrmacht 1943–45

Wehrmacht Uniforms

The main service uniform worn in the Wehrmacht was the Model 1936, which was specifically issued for battlefield conditions. This service uniform was field-grey in colour and manufactured from wool/rayon mixed material. It had four box-pleated pockets with a single metal finish button sewn to each of the four three pocket flaps. There were also five metal buttons sewn down the front of the tunic. The collar of the tunic was faced with dark blue-green material and sewn into this was the German Army collar patch indicating NCOs and other ranks. The shoulder straps made from dark blue-green material were sewn into the shoulders of the tunic at the arm end and positioned at the other with a single metal button. This allowed easy access to unpin the shoulder strap in order for the soldier to remove and replace it, pending of course on the wearer's rank as well as his branch of service. The shoulder strap could also be used to hold the soldiers military equipment in place on the shoulders.

The ends of the sleeves of the tunic were not cuff turned and were specially cut in order that the sleeve ends could be wrapped tighter around the soldier's wrist and this allowed it to be buttoned into position.

Stitched on the right of the tunic above the breast pocket was the national emblem of Germany. This silver emblem consisted of an eagle with outstretched wings clutching on its claws a wreath containing a swastika. Another item of cloth normally sewn onto the uniform was the German Army rank chevron and occasionally the specialist insignia, trade and specialist badge. These items were sewn directly onto the left sleeve of the field service uniform without any backing cloth. All types of arm rank chevrons and specialist badges were worn on the upper left arm of the uniform tunic, the service and field service tunics as well as the greatcoats.

The Model 1936 service uniform was worn throughout the war but by 1942, with still no sign of the war coming to a victorious conclusion, the manufacturing industry began to lack the basic uniform materials needed to support the clothing of millions of soldiers on the battlefield. As a result of these problems forced upon the overstretched German economy manufacturers designed a new model service tunic called the Model 1943 or M1943. The design of the M1943 uniform no longer had box-pleated pockets, nor did it have dark blue-green collar material. Instead it was made in field-grey cloth. Generally though the uniform was very similar to that of the M1936, but the quality was poor. The wearer also complained that the tunic was not well insulated and became very heavy when subjected to sustained down pours of rain.

In spite of the shoddy appearance of the new M1943 service uniform, it was generally hard wearing and was worn by thousands of soldiers during this period of the war. However, by 1944 with the German Army embroiled on both the Eastern and Western Fronts, manufacturers became even harder pressed to mass-produce service uniforms with the pressures put on them by the constant economic restraints of the war. Despite these problems by September 1944, a completely revised style of field service uniform was rushed into production, the model 1944 or M1944.

The M1944 service uniform was radically different from the traditional German Army uniform worn, and designers had actually adopted the style very similar to that of the British Army uniform blouse. The colour of the uniform was grey-green. The jacket had two large pockets without pleats but with pocket flaps, which was fastened by a single metal button. There were six buttons worn down the front. The German national emblem was still worn on the right breast above the pocket. There were shoulder straps displaying the wearer's rank and the cuffs to the sleeves were designed very similar to that of the standard German army service tunic. The collar was of the same material as the blouse and was in the late pattern mouse-grey colour.

The M1944 became a very popular service uniform during the last year of the war and was worn by both the German army and the *Waffen-SS*. Non-commissioned officers and commissioned officers including Generals did wear the M1944, but these slightly differed from the standard design. Non-commissioned officers rarely wore any rank braiding around the edge of the collar, and the only indication of their rank was their shoulder straps. Generals though wore the collar patches and normal rank insignia. However, their M1944 uniforms differed slightly in style, which included two breast patch pockets that had box pleats and curved edges to the flap pockets, and the buttons were not visible down the front of the blouse because it had been made with a fly front.

One of the last items of clothing to be worn during the war, which was regarded as a service uniform, was the reed-green denim field service uniform. This was introduced in the summer of 1944 and was a very successful and popular uniform worn by soldiers on the front lines, but could also be worn by non-commissioned officers as well. Both the jacket and the trousers were lightweight and hard wearing and were of matching reed green herringbone pattern denim. The jacket had four patch pockets and ten field-grey metal buttons, six of which were positioned down the front of the jacket and one to each pocket. The garment carried the normal insignia. The trousers to the uniform were in the normal field-grey colour and were in the same style and quality to that of the jacket.

For the second winter of 1942 a German Army reversible winter uniform was manufactured and supplied to the front lines. When the troops were issued with these garments in October and November 1942, they found the clothing extremely warm and comfortable. The uniform also provided the wearer with greater freedom of movement, especially with personal equipment. This uniform not only helped combat the severity of the cold, but helped prevent overheating during physical exertion.

The reversible clothing itself consisted of a heavy reversible double-breasted over jacket that was designed for extra frontal warmth. It had double buttoned overlaps to the flaps of the jacket to the front, which when closed were wind resistant. The bottom edge of the jacket had drawstrings attached, and the ends of the cuffs were also adjustable as well. The trousers worn were thick, as was the jacket, and was completely reversible. They were shorter in length to normal standard issue uniformed trousers but could be either worn over the top of the leather marching boots or tucked inside. The ends of the trousers were gathered in by drawstrings and tied in around the boots.

The winter reversible was normally mouse-grey on one side and winter white on the other. The soldiers wore the reversible garment pending on the terrain. If the area was snow covered the wearer wore the uniform on the winter white side out, and during operations where the was no snow, it was worn mouse-grey side out. However, there were other variations of the reversible, which included the green splinter pattern and the tan water pattern.

The reversible uniform was designed large enough to be worn over the service uniform, including personal equipment. However, troops did favour wearing most of their equipment over the winter jacket.

For the next four years of the war the German soldier was seen wearing these popular winter camouflage garments. By the early winter of 1943, the winter reversible had become one of the most popular items of winter clothing worn by the troops. Soldier survivability had actually increased, in spite of the major military setbacks. In the winter of 1941 more than half the cases of casualties were caused by the extreme sub-zero temperatures like frostbite. By the end of 1942, this figure had reduced considerably. A year later in the winter of 1943, it was less than a quarter of the casualties.

Panzer & Assault Gun Uniforms

The Panzer uniform remained a well-liked and very popular item of clothing and did not alter extensively during the war. However, in 1942 a special two-piece reed-green denim suit was issued to Panzer crews in areas of operations where the climate was considered warmer than normal theatres of combat. The new denim suit was hard wearing, light and easy to wash, and many crews were seen wearing the uniform during the summer months. The uniform was generally worn by armoured crews, maintenance, and even Panzergrenadiers who were operating with half tracked vehicles, notably the Sd.Kfz.251 series. This popular and practical garment was identical in cut to the special black Panzer uniform. It consisted of the normal insignia, including the national emblem, Panzer death head collar patches and shoulder straps.

Apart from the uniforms worn by the Panzer arm, crews of the armoured anti-tank units also initially wore the Panzer black uniform. However, with the increased need on the battlefield for self-propelled assault gun and tank destroyer units in close support of infantry, it was considered that the black Panzer uniform was unsuitable as crews were more exposed on the battlefield when they left their armoured vehicles. A special uniform was introduced for both *Sturmartillerie* and *Panzerjäger* units. The uniform was specially designed primarily to be worn inside and away from their armoured vehicles, and for this reason designers had produced a garment that gave better camouflage qualities than the standard black Panzer uniform. The uniform worn by units of the *Panzerjäger* was made entirely from lightweight grey-green wool material. The cut was very similar to that of the black Panzer uniform. However, it did differ in respect of insignia and the collar patches.

The *Panzerjäger* uniform was a very practical garment and it was identical to the cut of the to the *Sturmartillerie* uniform, but with the exception of the colour. The uniform was made entirely of field-grey cloth, but again differed in respect to certain insignia. The collar patches consisted of the death's head emblems, which were stitched on patches of dark blue-green cloth and were edged with bright red *Waffenfarbe* piping. However, officers did not display the death head collar patches, but wore the field service collar patches instead. No piping on the collar patches were used either.

Like the summer two-piece reed-green Panzer denim suit worn by Panzer crews, both tank destroyer and self-propelled assault gun units also had their own working and summer uniforms, which were also produced in the same colour and material.

With both the *Panzerjäger* and *Sturmartillerie* uniforms black leather marching boots were worn. The ends of the long trousers were worn over the boots and tied in around the lower calves. Short black ankle boots were also worn with the uniform.

Apart from the basic issued items of clothing worn by crews of the Panzer, tank destroyer and self-propelled assault gun units, crews were also issued with various items of clothing to protect them against the harsh climates. The first item issued was the standard grey-green greatcoat. Other items worn especially during the winter periods and when there was a heavy snowfall, was the winter white camouflage smocks. However, during the first winter of 1941/42 Panzer crews found both the camouflage smocks and Greatcoat difficult to wear, especially in the small confines of an armoured vehicle. Consequently, by the winter of 1942/43 the German Army had developed a new revolutionary item of clothing for the armoured crews called the parka. The parka was a well-made item of clothing that was well-padded and kept crews warm. Initially the parka was first designed in field-grey with a reversible winter white. But by late 1943 a new modification was made by replacing the field-grey side with a camouflage pattern, either in green splinter or tan water. The coat was double-breasted with the interior set of buttons being fastened to provide additional protection.

STEEL HELMET

The M1935 helmet evolved a number of times throughout war and the changes were primarily based on the growing wartime economic demands. Each modification resulted in a slightly newer variation although each helmet retained the basic design. At least three other models were manufactured exclusively for combat. However, the standard army issue steel helmet was the M1935 and later the M1943. The M1943 was more or less the same design as the M1935, but the shape of the helmet was slightly different and appeared larger around the base.

Generally the steel helmets issued to all German soldiers were usually field-grey in colour and were manufactured either in matt or semi-matt finishes. However, in hotter climates like North Africa, Italy and even during the summer months in southern Russia, soldiers over-painted their steel helmets in a sand base colour. Some helmets were painted very crudely, but this still ensured better camouflage than the standard field-grey appearance. In snow, soldiers found it necessary to apply white paint over the steel helmet. Initially, during the first winter of 1941, many troops did not attempt to apply their steel helmets with any type of white camouflage, often leaving them in the field-grey. However, some did attempt to find a solution in order for them to blend in with the local terrain. A number of soldiers found that chalk was very useful and applied this crudely over the entire helmet. But it was whitewash paint that became the most widely used form of winter camouflage. The use of whitewash paint was a very popular solution to winter camouflage and its idea came from the whitewashing of tanks and other armoured vehicles. Other forms of camouflaging steel helmets, pending on the season of course, were also used extensively by the Wehrmacht.

Ranks

GERMAN ARMY	WAFFEN-SS	BRITISH ARMY
Gemeiner, Landser	Schütze	Private
	Oberschütze	
Grenadier	Sturmmann	Lance Corporal
Obergrenadier		
Gefreiter	Rottenführer	Corporal
Obergefreiter	Unterscharführer	
Stabsgefreiter		
Unteroffizier	Scharführer	Sergeant
Unterfeldwebel	Oberscharführer	Colour Sergeant
Feldwebel		
Oberfeldwebel	Hauptscharführer	Sergeant Major
Stabsfeldwebel	Hauptbereitschaftsleiter	
	Sturmscharführer	Warrant Officer
Leutnant	Untersturmführer	Second Lieutenant
Oberleutnant	Obersturmführer	First Lieutenant
Hauptmann	Hauptsturmführer	Captain
Major	Sturmbannführer	Major
Oberstleutnant	Obersturmbannführer	Lieutenant Colonel
Oberst	Standartenführer	Colonel
	Oberführer	Brigadier General
Generalmajor	Brigadeführer	Major General
Generalleutnant	Gruppenführer	Lieutenant General
General	Obergruppenführer	General
Generaloberst	Oberstgruppenführer	
Generalfeldmarschall	Reichsführer-SS